Heidi Johnston has embarked on an enormously important task – to direct Christians of all ages to face up to the questions: 'What is **holiness**? How does it look in daily life? How can we cultivate lives that demonstrate this kind of holiness?' – and to realize that the answers are all there in Scripture – to be true followers of Jesus, allowing God's Word to transform our lives into true reflections of Christ's loveliness.

Dr Helen Roseveare, author, speaker and former missionary to the Congo

Deuteronomy, of all biblical books, can safely be left, can it not, to impractical students of ancient law? Heidi Johnston maintains the very opposite. Wife and mother of two daughters, she well knows the joys and struggles of family life, and writes from this perspective. But in this volume she enthusiastically records the particular passages throughout Deuteronomy that have brought her correction, comfort and stimulus, and the enticement of its ever-enlarging moral horizons. What a refreshing change this is.

Professor David Gooding, Professor Emeritus of Old Testament Greek, Queen's University, Belfast

Life
in the
Big
Story

To Dad
who taught me to fly

Life in the Big Story

Your place...

...in God's unfolding plan

Heidi Johnston

Foreword by Rebecca Manley Pippert

INTER-VARSITY PRESS
Norton Street, Nottingham NG7 3HR, England
Email: ivp@ivpbooks.com
Website: www.ivpbooks.com

First published 2012

British Library Cataloguing in Publication Data
A catalogue record for this book is available from the British Library.

ISBN: 978–1–84474–579–1

Set in Dante 12/15pt
Typeset in Great Britain by CRB Associates, Potterhanworth, Lincolnshire
Printed and bound in Great Britain by Ashford Colour Press Ltd, Gosport,
Hampshire

*Inter-Varsity Press publishes Christian books that are true to the Bible and that
communicate the gospel, develop discipleship and strengthen the church for its
mission in the world.*

*Inter-Varsity Press is closely linked with the Universities and Colleges Christian
Fellowship, a student movement connecting Christian Unions in universities and
colleges throughout Great Britain, and a member movement of the International
Fellowship of Evangelical Students. Website: www.uccf.org.uk*

Contents

Foreword

'The Universe is made of stories not of atoms' poet Muriel Rukeyser famously proclaimed. Stories are how we make sense of the world and our place in it. But is there a story that is big enough to build our lives upon? That gives our lives ultimate meaning and purpose? Heidi Johnston states in this remarkable book that our lives are never intended to be trivial. Rather they have greater meaning than we could ever possibly imagine.

But what is it that keeps us from the things we long for? How do we discover who we are and why we are here? Somehow we know we were made for something more. Something more seemed promised. There is more for us to live for, to embrace or be embraced by. We are surely here to participate in something wider and deeper than we have yet realized. We want to know that our lives are significant, that it will make a difference that we have been here.

Yet often our pursuit of happiness becomes our agony. It leaves us emptier and lonelier than ever. We are still left feeling wistful for something deeper that will satisfy our longing. But what is it that we want and how on earth are we to reach it?

Life in the Big Story takes both believers and seekers on a pilgrimage to discover the meaning of our individual stories – our identity, our purpose, our destiny – by helping us understand the big story; what has been called the greatest story ever told. Johnston shows us how the essential message of the biblical story, to paraphrase G. K. Chesterton, is the key that fits the lock of reality.

She begins by skilfully revealing how the story of dusty pilgrims walking towards the Promised Land 3,000 years ago has deep relevance to our fast-paced, frenetic twenty-first-century world. We learn that their story is our story. As she progresses to the life of Jesus, we learn not only what it means to be human, but with insightfulness and startling freshness, she helps us understand the person of Jesus, the meaning of his death and resurrection – and why it matters so much. When she moves to the story of the early church, once again we discover that their struggles and lessons are ours as well.

This is a lot to take on for a first book! But Johnston does it with considerable insight and an excitement that is positively contagious. She helps us see why the age-old, biblical narrative informs us who we are and whose we are. *Life in the Big Story* motivates us to take our place as children of God: radically transformed yet, as C. S. Lewis once wrote, leaving us more ourselves than we ever dreamt possible.

This book is for believers, who want to know how understanding the big story will bring meaning and ultimate purpose to their own individual story. And it is for seekers, who are willing to ask whether the wistful longings of the heart are actually within reach and not there to mock us.

On a personal note, one of the privileges during the time we have been living in Northern Ireland has been meeting and knowing the author. I know *her* story: counting as dear friends her beloved grandmother, parents, brother, in-laws, husband and children. That has made the reading of this book all the more meaningful and remarkable.

Becky Pippert
Holywood, N. Ireland

Acknowledgments

Thanks to:

Sam Parkinson, Kate Byrom and everyone at Inter-Varsity Press. Thank you for not only taking a risk on an unknown writer, but for the rare blend of godliness and professionalism which made the whole process so enjoyable.

Rebecca Manley Pippert and her husband Dick for your support and encouragement. It is a privilege to be part of your Northern Irish family!

Desi Maxwell, from whose sources I have borrowed liberally and whose passion for God's word has kindled my own.

Valerie Murphy for your friendship and guidance, and for reminding me so many times that we have an awesome God who can and will do things which are beyond our wildest imaginings.

Stephen and Ruth Shaw for your encouragement and friendship, your invaluable help with proof-reading and for showing me what logic on fire looks like.

The church family at Scrabo, where I have found real friendship and a spiritual home. Your faithfulness and devotion to God humble me on so many levels. Special thanks to everyone in the Precept group for pushing me to go deeper and for making me part of your Haverim.

Tom and Jean for your encouragement and support and for welcoming me into your family. Granny Sherrard for a lifetime of holding fast and the steadfast faith that continues to be an inspiration. Andrew, not only my little brother but a valued friend whose wisdom never ceases to amaze me.

Mum and Dad, you have given me roots and wings, love and laughter, friendship, unwavering support and an insight into the heart of God which has coloured my life from the earliest moments. For that there are not enough words to say thank you.

Ellie and Lara, being your mum is an adventure that brings so much joy into my life. You continue to astonish me on a daily basis and I have already learned more from you than you will ever know. I love you both.

Glenn, you see me at my worst and continue to love me, and that in itself is a gift I will never deserve. Thank you for being the husband I would have prayed for if I'd had the wisdom to know exactly what I needed and the faith to think big. It is an honour to share the journey with you.

And most importantly you, my God and Father, the one who makes my soul sing. The riches of life in your presence take my breath away and neither my words nor the love of my faltering heart could ever do justice to the wonder that is you.

Introduction

I had always felt life first as a story and if
there is a story there is a storyteller.
(G. K. Chesterton)[1]

Let me ask you a question. If someone asked you to tell your story, where would you begin? Would you start in a hospital with the chatter of family and the rustling of presents, as your beaming parents placed on you their hopes for the future? Perhaps for you life began more quietly and without the fanfare, with less love and a lot less dreaming? Maybe you grew up believing you would scale mountains, score goals, discover cures, conquer evil, love passionately and live your dreams? Somewhere deep down, was there a feeling that your story was going to be big? That it mattered what you did, whom you loved and what you believed in?

We want our story to count. We want our lives to make a difference. The problem for most of us is that, amid happiness, despair, promises kept or broken and perhaps even the odd glimpse of greatness, our stories have turned out smaller than we hoped.

On a global scale my story doesn't seem to amount to much. I am a daughter, a wife, a mother, a sister, a friend. I am privileged to have people around me who love me but most people will never know my name. Some day no-one will remember that I loved fajitas and hated soggy bread or that I kept a blue teddy bear from my childhood. No-one will know what made me laugh, or cry, or what memories I treasured most. If my story is the centre of my world then there is a smallness to life that denies all the hope I felt as a child. If I am all that matters then growing up teaches me only that life, at best, is disappointing.

If life is so small then why is it that the stories we see on movie screens, or read in books, or hear in songs, resonate so deeply? Why, again and again, do we crave stories of adventure, where passionate heroes fight and win when all seems lost? Where people find their purpose and refuse to give up whatever the cost? Where good triumphs over evil against all odds? Is it all just a futile attempt to take us outside ourselves, to indulge the wish that life had turned out differently, to live for a moment in the fantasy of what could have been? Or could there be another reason? Could it be that these moments are glimpses of a true story that has been written on our hearts since the beginning of time?

Let me ask you another question. What would change if your story was bigger than the life you live from day to day? If your story began before time and will continue when time ends? What if who you are and what you believe and the things you do matter on a scale you can't imagine? What if the dreams we had as children are actually the echo of something that has been planted within us by the very creator of the world?

If you discovered that your story could really change the world, what would it mean to you?

The story I have found myself in has changed me forever. It has introduced me to a God whose heart has captivated me,

INTRODUCTION | 19

whose mercy has humbled me and whose grace has given me a purpose for my life. It has taught me who I am.

I began to discover my story in what seemed a most unlikely place – the book of Deuteronomy. Tired and dusty, the children of Israel stand before Moses. Their history has been colourful already. Their hearts are beating wildly as they wait for a command that will change their lives forever. Ready to put the long years of waiting and wandering behind them, they prepare to take possession of the land they have been promised. As they listen, poised between what they are and all that they could be, the God of Israel begins to speak. In those moments, even before they set foot in Canaan, they hear what it means to belong to God. What it means to be a chosen people. They hear the call to live as part of a greater kingdom.

As I read, it slowly dawned on me that their story was, literally, my story. That their God was my God. You may wonder what makes it my story. Why should the lives of a group of Israelites, more than 3,000 years ago, have any impact on my glossy, fast-paced twenty-first-century world? To understand why their story is my story, we need to understand something about biblical Hebrew. If you open a Hebrew lexicon and search for the word 'history', you will find that it does not appear.[2] At first glance that presents a problem. With no word for history how do you delve into the past? How do you take lives that have long since ended and glean from them lessons for your own?

History was one of the subjects I enjoyed most at school. I was fascinated as I discovered the stories of civilizations past, of generations who had gone before me and what life had meant for them. I found myself drawn by their lives, momentarily led by my imagination into their world. The problem, twenty years later, is that I remember very little.

In contrast I have discovered that, while facts about the lives of people I never knew have faded from my mind, memories from my own life remain. If I'm honest, the reason for that is simple. My story means more to me than the history of others.

While their story is history, mine is memory.

Which brings me back to the Hebrew Bible. The word history does not appear because, for the people of God, the biblical story is more than just history. When we open the Bible to the book of Genesis, Exodus or even Deuteronomy, we are not reading the history of a distant nation, we are discovering our story. We are drawn into the *memory*[3] of the kingdom of which we are part. The history of others may interest or even teach us, but it is our own story that shapes us. Memory is part of who we are.

It makes sense then, that in order to understand who I am and who I was created to be, I must go back to the beginning. This is the journey on which I have found myself.

The journey from history to memory.
The journey that made their story my story.
The journey that transformed the Bible from dry fact to living truth.
The journey that brought me into the presence of a God whose love was as evident in the awesome holiness of the Old Testament as it was in the person of Jesus, holiness incarnate.

If, as I did, you have always assumed the book of Deuteronomy to be dry and unappealing, then to mention it risks tempting you to close this book and choose another. That's probably what I would have done. However, as someone who almost missed its treasures myself, may I encourage you to stay for a while? As we linger for a few chapters and uncover the heart of Deuteronomy, you will begin to understand why it has profoundly changed my life and, more importantly, why it was the book quoted most often by Jesus. Like me, I hope what you discover will deepen your understanding of God, as well as what we are called to as his people. This is not a story simply to warm your heart, although it will. It is not just a story to show that you belong, which you do. It is a call to take your place as a child of God and live a life that is radically transformed. A life that demonstrates the marriage of holiness and love. Far from the distant irrelevant list of laws I had assumed it to be, it is a living, vibrant kingdom manifesto penned by a God whose heartbeat is the very sound of hope.

While we will pause for a while to hear the challenge God laid before his people as they prepared to enter the Promised Land, it is only a part of our story. As we move on we will come, perhaps with a fresh understanding, to the life of Jesus. Putting flesh on the words he had spoken through Moses all those years ago, the God of Sinai showed what it meant to be human and yet live with the song of a different kingdom ringing in your heart. Jesus reminded his people again that to belong to God is the very highest of callings.

The death and resurrection of Jesus was neither the end of one story nor the beginning of another. Just as we do, the early church found themselves living in a new chapter of an age-old story which was bigger than they dared imagine. A chapter that was different, yet inseparable from all that had gone before. Armed with the memory of the kingdom, the words of writers like Paul can help us find our place in this epic story. As he writes with contagious excitement to the church in Ephesus we discover that the people of every generation, wherever they are in time and history, are called to hear the heartbeat of God and let it transform their own.

If you honour me with your company, we will journey together through some of this story and ask a few questions along the way.

- Why did God choose a specific set of people?
- What was his relationship with them?
- How did he want them to live and why did it matter?
- What changed when Jesus came?
- Where do I fit into the story?
- If all this is true, how does it change the way I live?

After his resurrection, Jesus walked with two disciples on the road to Emmaus, explaining to them the wonder and reality of the story that has always led to him. My prayer is that you, like them, will find your heart begins to burn within you. That you will be reminded, or perhaps discover for the first time, the joy, the solemnity and the awesome privilege of being part of a people called by God.

Discussion questions

1. In Ecclesiastes 3:11 God is described as having 'set eternity in the hearts of men'. How could this help us understand our hunger for significance? In what ways do people today misinterpret this longing?
2. In 1 Corinthians 10:1, Paul refers to the Old Testament characters as *our* forefathers. Given that he is writing to Gentile (non-Jewish) believers, why does he use the word *our*? What would change if we viewed the Old Testament as our story, rather than simply history?

3. Read Luke 24:13–27. What Scriptures did Jesus use to explain his death and resurrection? In verse 32, how were the men affected by his words? How does Jesus' approach to the Old Testament compare with that of the church in general today? Why?

4. Do you see your life as part of a bigger story? How could an understanding of the big story impact your own individual story?

1 The back story

Then he [Jesus] started at the beginning,
with the books of Moses, and went on through
all the prophets, pointing out everything
in the Scriptures that referred to him.
(Luke 24:27 MSG)

Imagine for a moment you find yourself in a room with two men. One is thin and pale, the beating of his heart the only sound in the charged silence. Another man stands over him. This man is taller, with a strength that only highlights the weakness of the first. His masked face barely disguises the clenched muscles in his jaw and beads of sweat begin to break across his forehead. As you watch, he takes a knife and deliberately plunges it into the other's chest.

How do you feel towards the masked man? Anger? Fear? Revulsion? A man who attacks the helpless must surely have the coldest heart.

What if I told you that the mask was the mask of a surgeon, worn to protect the man whose life he is preparing to save? What if the knife was a scalpel and the weakness of the other was the result of an aggressive and deadly cancer, silently stealing a life it was never meant to take?

Do your feelings change?

Perhaps I can go further. What if the beads of sweat are not just the result of the intense concentration of the surgeon, but of his inner turmoil. Because of his skill and years of experience, the surgeon is the only one qualified to perform this operation, which is why he finds himself ready to lower his scalpel and cut into the body of his own son.

The more you understand this story, the more your appreciation of the father grows. Instead of revulsion and horror you begin to feel respect and admiration. Armed with the full story you can begin to sense the pain of a father as he does what is necessary to save his child, holding back nothing in his determination to stop the spread of the cancer that will ultimately rob his son of life.

Many of us live our Christian lives in the first paragraph of this story. We see the 'God of the Old Testament' as a distant power, unpredictable, harsh, sometimes even vengeful. Only when we begin to explore his word, to really see his heart, do we realize that the God whose face seemed hidden from his people is the God whose love sent Jesus to deal, once and for all, with the deadly sin that kept us from him and robbed us of the life we were created to have. The God who came as one of us, removed the mask that had protected us from glory we could not endure and allowed us to see him. It is often when we skip straight to the part we have deemed important or relevant that we find ourselves struggling to understand truth, much less apply it.

Often in our home, particularly over dinner, there is a lot of competition to share the events of the day. Usually my daughters, Ellie and Lara, are each trying to get in first to tell us about some incident at school or with their friends.

Lara, the younger of the two, has developed an interesting approach to this. Instead of taking up time with detail she considers irrelevant, she jumps straight to the best part of the story. The problem is, although she gets there quickly, the rest of us have no idea what she is talking about. Rather than entering into and enjoying her story, we all end up confused and lost. Inevitably my husband will say, 'Lara, we need the back story!'

Like Lara, many people have a tendency to jump straight into the pages of Matthew, to attempt to understand the coming of Jesus without the light of what has gone before. The grave danger in doing so is that we would end up at best baffled and at worst seriously misinformed. If we want to understand the story we must begin at the beginning, or as the Greeks would have called it, the 'genesis'.

In the beginning was God. Not created, not appearing, but already there. Before anything there was God, Father, Son and Holy Spirit, existing in a perfect three-way relationship that was the very source and expression of love. Before people there was relationship, already at the heart of the character of God.

Out of the life that existed only within that perfect relationship, God created man in his own image. Within man was the potential to love, to create, to feel joy and to walk in relationship with each other and with the God who breathed him into life. Mankind's deep desire for relationship would find its home as they walked in intimacy with God.

As they enjoyed his presence, God gave man a job that fulfilled his very nature, entrusting him with the care of the creation that reflected God's glory. In their book, *The Drama of Scripture*, Craig Bartholomew and Michael Goheen illustrate man's intended role in God's creation like this:

Imagine that you are a fifteenth-century sculptor and one day receive an email from Michelangelo himself, asking if you would be willing to come to his studio and complete a piece of work he has begun. He mentions that you are expected to continue the work in such a way that Michelangelo's own reputation will be enhanced by the finished product! God's call to us to 'have dominion' over his creation entails this sort of compliment to what we are capable of achieving as his stewards.[1]

Man was created in the image of God and would find deep satisfaction in his presence and the work that gave expression to that relationship with God. That relationship was designed to go on forever, without decaying or breaking down in any way.

Alongside all the love, creativity and uniqueness that were poured into man was another characteristic on which this relationship with God hinged. The freedom to choose. God was not a task master or even a scientist who created robots to serve him. From the beginning, mankind would always have a choice. To walk with God or to walk alone. By Genesis 3 we had chosen to walk alone.

When I was a child it seemed harsh, even cruel, that the whole of mankind should be punished because Eve, whom I had never met, took a bite of some fruit she wasn't allowed. It seemed a monumental overreaction to a pretty minor offence. The truth is, it wasn't about the fruit. God had provided everything that Adam and Eve would ever need, and abundantly more. The question they faced was the same one that hangs tantalizingly before each of us every moment of every day. Does God really know what's best for me? Is there something better out there if I do it my way? As Eve reached for the fruit, the choice she made was less about food and more about the voice she would choose to guide her life. And so began man's quest to try to live without God.

Armed with rebellious hearts it was no longer possible for people to live in perfect relationship with God. As heaven groaned, Adam and Eve were clothed tenderly and taken out of the garden, and away from their source of life. You see, without God, living forever was no longer possible. The God who loved his people would not allow them to suffer endlessly the consequences of their own stubborn choices. Without him, their desires would go unsatisfied and their hearts would ache with an unquenchable emptiness. To live like that forever would be pain without end. In the words of C. S. Lewis, 'God can't give us peace and happiness apart from himself because there is no such thing.'[2] Life without God is not life at all.

And so, for the first time, death was a reality and the life mankind had once enjoyed became a memory that whispered restlessly in the corners of their hearts. A memory that would prepare them for the time when God would come for them. He would go to unimaginable lengths to restore their broken relationship and give them back the life for which they were created.

Before he did that there were lessons to be learned. Before he would come to them, he would teach them who he was and who they were meant to be. He would show them what it meant to be his.

To do that he chose Israel.

There are a few questions I have asked again and again when it comes to the nation of Israel. Questions like, why them? What was it about Israel that caused God to choose them? Why did he seem to love them more than everyone else? Did God not care about the other nations?

Somewhere deep down, although I would never have admitted it, I suspected that God had a tendency to act like a cruel father who picks a favourite child, heartlessly disregarding the others. The problem was that this idea sat completely at odds with the God whose heart is so evident in other parts of the Bible. How could this God of love care so much for some people and so little for others? In fact, if this could be true, can I ever be sure he cares about me?

As I came to understand a little of the role of Israel in God's plan, the truth began to dawn on me. God chose Israel, not because he didn't care about the other nations, but because he did. Not because he was selective in his love but because he was love itself. As he looked at the people he had created he loved them with the love of a father who longs for his wayward child to come home.

The sad reality was that very quickly, only a few chapters into the story of mankind, Eden had been all but forgotten. Although the ache was still there, people no longer recognized it for what it was. In the midst of the mess they had made, mankind had forgotten what it meant to walk with God. Before he would clear the way for them to come home they had to be reminded. Somehow, outside Eden, they had to see what it was like to live with purpose as the people of God. The Israelites were not chosen because of who they were, but because of who he is. As Jonathan Sacks explains,

> God asks one individual, eventually a family, a tribe, a
> collection of tribes, a nation to serve as an exemplary role
> model, to be as it were a living case study in what it is to live
> continuously in the presence of God.[3]

Israel would be God's light in a very dark world, displaying to that world something of the glory of the one true God. Knowing him, walking with him and living his heart.

In order to build a nation who would walk as he led, God began with a man who was prepared to follow him even when he didn't know where he was going. He would risk everything that represented security, protection and even identity to walk with God. That man was Abraham.

God promised Abraham, a childless man of seventy-five whose wife was unable to conceive, that he would have descendants more numerous than the stars that filled every inch of the desert sky stretching above his head. The family that began with him would not only be great, but through them would come a blessing which would change the world. Not only that, God promised that he would give Abraham's family a land of their own. A place to call home, where they could live and work and grow. A place where they could learn to walk in the presence of the God they were only beginning to know. In order to seal these promises, to give Abraham the assurance that they were unbreakable, God made a covenant.

The closest thing we have to a covenant as Abraham would have known it is probably marriage, and even that comparison is flawed. I heard of a conversation that took place recently in a hair salon close to where I live. The young woman who was having her hair cut was beaming from ear to ear and, as she chatted to the hairdresser, it transpired that she was in love. Bubbling over with enthusiasm, she confided that she had made an appointment to get a tattoo with her boyfriend's name and was considering getting married. Pausing for a moment the hairdresser replied, 'If you are in love, I can understand getting married, but isn't a tattoo a bit permanent?'

In the twenty-first century, where promises are so often made and broken, where clauses are found to set aside contracts and marriage vows are often trampled on, it can be hard to grasp the solemn significance of such a covenant. For

Abraham the significance was profound. He understood that by making a covenant, God was entering into a binding, unbreakable agreement that was as secure as the life of God himself.

Abraham saw the result of some of God's promises in his lifetime, others he saw only by faith. At the age of 100 God gave him the promised son, whose name was Isaac. Isaac had a son whose name was Jacob. Jacob, after he met with God, had his name changed to 'Israel'. Jacob had twelve sons, who grew into twelve tribes, who grew into the nation that would carry the name Israel from that point on. As time passed the covenant God made with Abraham was passed down from generation to generation. It was this covenant, written on the heart of God, which gave them hope even in their darkest days.

Even when the Israelites found themselves enslaved in Egypt, God's fingerprints were evident. When they were forced into submission, backs breaking under the weight of the loads they carried, their pain was felt by the God who loved them and, as he promised, there came a point when he would let it go on no longer.

When God used Moses to lead the Israelites out of Egypt he did so much more than simply rescue them. By defeating the might of Pharaoh, with his gods and his power and his status, he made it clear that he alone was God. By fulfilling his promises he reminded his people that he was faithful and that their lives were safe in his hands.

The exodus, as we have come to know it, was significant for so many reasons. When the judgment of God finally fell on Egypt he offered protection to those who, by painting the blood of a lamb on the doorposts and lintel of their house, were prepared to put their trust in his promise. As the Israelites crossed the Red Sea and left behind the slavery of Egypt, imprinted on their minds was the image of a lamb that took their place. The feast of Passover was embedded into the fabric of the nation so that, centuries later, when a man who claimed to be God described himself as the 'lamb of God' the significance was beyond anything our western ears immediately grasp. When that same man was killed at Passover, his blood running down the beams of a wooden cross, an even greater rescue was taking place, not just for Israel but for the world.

Rescued from slavery, the nation of Israel were led under God's protection to the foot of Mount Sinai. There the God who had once more proved his faithfulness spoke to them through Moses, saying,

> You yourselves have seen what I did to the Egyptians, and
> how I bore you on eagles' wings, and *brought you to myself*.
> Now then, if you will indeed obey my voice and keep my
> covenant, then you shall be my own possession among all
> the peoples, for all the earth is mine; and you shall be to me
> a kingdom of priests and a holy nation.
> (Exodus 19:4–6, my emphasis)

In the shadow of Mount Sinai, before they began their journey to the land that God had prepared for them, another covenant was made. They knew from experience that God was utterly faithful, but this time the people had a part to play. This time the blessings that God promised to pour over them depended on their obedience. In those moments God began to lay out for them the life that is worthy of his kingdom. As the mountain blazed and shook with his glory, the people heard his voice and trembled in the presence of the awesome God who had called them to be his.

Why did God remain a part of the story of mankind, even after they turned their backs on him? Why did he make the covenant with Abraham? Why did he protect his people for centuries, watch over them in Egypt and finally rescue them in power and lead them to Sinai? He did it to bring them to himself. He did it to bring them back into the relationship that had always been their home. For a moment at Sinai they had a glimpse of the people they were created to be. A glimpse of what had been for a heartbeat in Eden and could be again forever.

The plan God had for the people he loved was so much more than just release from slavery. They were not simply set free from what had been, they were called to something more. As will always be true for God's people, freedom was not the end result but the beginning of a journey with God that would transform their lives and lead them home.

Discussion questions

1. How will a limited understanding of the Bible impact our view of God? What dangers are we leaving ourselves open to?

2. What was man's original created purpose? How was this purpose affected by the Genesis story? What problem did mankind now face?

3. Why did God choose to have a special covenant relationship with the nation of Israel? What was Israel's responsibility?

4. Read 1 Peter 2:9. In what ways are the role of the church today similar to the one God gave the nation of Israel? How will God's instructions to Israel help us fulfil the role he has given us?

2 Why bother with obedience?

We know that we have come to know him
if we obey his commands.
(1 John 2:3)

The scene is set as a hush falls across the plains of Moab. The air almost crackles with the charged anticipation of a nation who are ready to cross the Jordan into their new home. As the excitement builds the Israelites know that the waiting is almost at an end. Now, before they move forward, Moses prepares to lay their story before them one more time.

The expectant faces that look back at him this time are different. Gone are the men and women who strode, triumphant, out of Egypt. A new generation stand ready to hear the words of their God but, before they do, Moses reminds them of the forty years that have passed since their parents stood at Mount Sinai.

This is not the first time the nation of Israel have stood on the border of the Promised Land. Fresh from their dramatic rescue and their experiences at Sinai, it took only eleven days for God to bring his people to the edge of their inheritance.

Just as he promised, the land had been theirs for the taking.
All they had to do was go in and possess it. The God who
displayed his power in Egypt had already fought for them in
every battle they faced. The God who heard the cry of their
hearts and freed them from slavery had cared for them in the
wilderness and led them on every step of their journey. Going
before them, he had prepared even the hearts of their enemies
so that victory was secure. Despite all this, Deuteronomy 1:32
tells us that the Israelites refused to trust. Choosing to see the
size of the enemy instead of the power of their God, they
turned and walked away from all that he had offered them.

In that moment, the God who would have been their
protector became instead their judge. The people who should
have enjoyed his favour felt instead his anger. Disobedience
cost a generation their inheritance. Yes, they were still the
people of God and could know him in the desert, but what
blessing they forfeited.

Instead of growing up in the Promised Land, the generation
who stand before Moses now were raised as nomads. For forty
years they wandered in the desert, until eventually every one
of the disbelieving generation had died. Deuteronomy is the
call of God to a new generation who are tired of the desert
and ready to live. Even during forty years of wandering their
experience of God had only served to confirm his faithfulness
and the moment they longed for had finally come. Now, on
the plains of Moab, it was their turn to choose.

There are times when God chooses a seemingly ordinary
moment to bring home the reality of our relationship with
him. For me, one such moment happened during a car journey
with my father-in-law. I don't remember where we were going
or why. I don't remember what had happened in the hours
before we left but I remember clearly how I felt. Whatever
my children had done, I was not happy. As we drove I recounted

the events of the day, my indignation building as the story progressed. Despite the fact that I love and want the best for them, my daughters seemed determined to do exactly the opposite of what I asked. By the time I had finished talking I was wound up and ready to explode. In a moment of vented frustration I turned to my father-in-law and barked these words: 'Do you think they will they ever just do what I ask without fighting me at every turn?' In the silence that followed it occurred to me that God could often ask that question of me.

The book of Deuteronomy is in many ways a call for the children of Israel to answer the same question. Will they ever simply do what God asks without fighting him at every turn? Will they understand that his law is for their good and their protection? As they listen again to the words of a God who loves them relentlessly, will they realize that obedience really does matter?

In his last days with the people he loves, Moses speaks with the urgency of a man who knows his God and understands the profound significance of the words he is about to speak. He knows the choice they will make is literally a matter of life and death.

It is against this backdrop that he sets out for them the law of God, beginning with these words, 'Hear now, O Israel, the decrees and laws I am about to teach you. Follow them so that you may live and may go in and take possession of the land that the LORD, the God of your fathers, is giving you' (Deuteronomy 4:1).

Perhaps it seems a strange place to start. As they embark on the adventure that is their very purpose in life, why begin by talking about the law? Why not start with a celebration? He begins with the law because, if they were going to play their part in the story God was writing, they had to understand the life to which he was calling them. If they were going to live in the fullness they were created for, fulfilling their purpose as the people of God, then that first flush of excitement had to translate into the practical obedience of life in his kingdom.

I think one reason we struggle to understand the relationship the Israelites had with God's law comes from our perception of law itself. We tend to view it as dry and restrictive, a necessary evil we must obey to avoid punishment. Having studied law for five years at university, I am more than familiar with the problem. Sitting in the library, surrounded by books on conveyancing and intellectual property law, I would have struggled to put the words law and joy together! I first came to God's law with the same mindset, only to discover that it is something entirely different. If we are going to understand how the law could be a demonstration of the heart of God, we must learn to see it as the Israelites did.

The Hebrew word for law is Torah,[1] meaning instruction or direction. The word Torah comes originally from another verb, *yarah*,[2] which as well as meaning to instruct or teach can also mean to shoot or take aim. Taking these meanings together we can begin to understand how the Jewish people view the law or 'Torah' of God. Rather than a restrictive set of rules they see a body of teaching, given by a loving God, intended to guide them into the full and blessed life that can be theirs in him. By beginning their new life with the law, God was not restricting their freedom but celebrating it and urging them to fulfil the potential offered by this new life with him. The reading of the law was in fact a celebration of all they were now free to be.

As we consider God's plans for his people and the role of his law in that plan, it is important to understand this distinction. When we talk about the law of God we are not referring to something intended to be burdensome, but to Torah with all the richness and positive beauty the word invoked in the Jewish mind.

The Torah that God gave to Israel was in stark contrast to the law of other cultures. Rather than vengeance, it spoke of justice. Rather than being burdensome and in favour of the powerful, it was a law of equality and compassion that spoke volumes about its maker. As the Israelites observed his statutes they would come to know their God. When they kept his commandments they walked with him. To obey his law was to discover his heart.

While God called Israel to know him and live in relationship with him, he also called them to show the world who he is. As they lived in obedience in the Promised Land the people of God would also begin to live out their purpose as a light to the world around them. In verses 6–8 Moses points out three things that would not only result from obedience in the lives of the Israelites, but would be evidence to the surrounding nations of the presence and character of their God:

1. The wisdom and understanding of the Israelite nation.
2. The closeness of their relationship with God.
3. The practical effectiveness of the law itself.

Wisdom is a commodity that can be as lacking today as it is sorely needed. Often we make the mistake of confusing intellect with wisdom but the two are not the same. According to the Collins English Dictionary, wisdom is 'the ability to use one's experience and knowledge to make sensible decisions or judgements'. The Hebrew word refers to practical wisdom, as opposed to mere intellectual reasoning. As Marvin Wilson explains in his wonderful book, *Our Father Abraham*, 'For them [Hebrews], truth was not so much an idea to be contemplated as an experience to be lived.'[3] For the people of God, wisdom is not simply the ability to think but the capacity to apply the word of God to a life that was designed by him in the first place.

The idea that you must be academic to be wise came entirely from the Greeks and would have been alien to both the Jews of Deuteronomy and those of Jesus' day. Wisdom is not the proof of a superior intellect but the product of an obedient heart. When God became man he chose not to be a philosopher but a carpenter, a man whose practical life was infused with the heart and wisdom of God. The Israelites recognized that true wisdom grows in the nuts and bolts of daily living as God's standards are accepted and lived out. It grows when real people, whatever their nature or academic ability, commit themselves to knowing God and allow him to shape their moments, their days and gradually their lives.

The second result of the Israelites' obedience would be the closeness of their relationship with God. Unlike the God of Israel, the gods who were worshipped by the surrounding nations were seen as fickle. Their favour was sought through all manner of practices including ritual prostitution and even child sacrifice. In order to gain the favour of the gods, in the hope that they could hear, the people would offer exhausting supplications. Despite their fervour and continued effort there was no assurance that their gods would answer, or even that they were there at all.

In contrast stood Israel and her God. A God who answered his children when they called. A God who wanted the best for his people, delighting to bless them when they walked with him. A God with the heart of a father, in whose presence his people could rest.

In a world where the pursuit of success, wealth and even happiness is relentless, where exhaustion and stress are the norm, do those around you see a person who is at rest in the presence of their God? The contentment that comes in God's presence will not go unnoticed by a world that longs for peace it can never seem to find. If God's glory was to be revealed through the Israelites it would happen in their day-to-day lives, as they encountered real pressures and placed them with faith in the hands of a real God.

The third result of obedience would be to prove the practical effectiveness of God's law itself. I remember being given a little book full of advice on raising children. The contents of the book were helpful but the thing that struck me most was the story of the author. While she was a Christian, most of her invitations to lecture on the subject came from companies and organizations who had no religious affiliation. Her material proved so effective that she was repeatedly asked where it had been sourced. I could almost hear her chuckle as she described the look of shock that generally came over the faces of her audience when she revealed that her source was the Bible.

The legitimacy and effectiveness of God's pattern for life comes as a surprise to a lot of people. We live in a world that is desperately searching for answers to problems that seem to be getting out of control. It is almost impossible to open a newspaper without reading about the breakdown of the family unit or the decline in respect for others, yet these issues and so many more are at the heart of God's plan for his people. If God's word deals with the challenges that face our world, then it is time we shared it with a generation who are lost for answers. Why, when the important questions are being asked, does the church so often stay silent? Instead of providing a living example of practical obedience to the word of God, we absorb ourselves in television programmes and cultural norms. Instead of committing ourselves to knowing his word and living with confidence by the standards we find there, we take our direction from people who are as confused as we are.

Just as God's law would be honoured by Israel's obedience, the standards of God's kingdom will be vindicated when his people today are not afraid to live lives that are governed by obedience to his word.

For the Israelites, obedience was not an optional part of the story but the key to finding their place within it. The choice they faced sits before us with no less importance. As we stand with the people of Israel contemplating the implications of the obedience they are called to, we cannot ignore the importance of obedience in our own lives.

Obedience is not a word that sits well in the twenty-first-century mind. We are more at ease talking about our rights or being urged to take control of our own destiny. By its very nature, obedience takes us out of the driver's seat, yet it is the first thing God asks of those who want to find their place in his story.

Until we choose obedience we can never know God the way he intends or live the lives for which we were made. Not only that, unless our lives are marked by obedience, the people around us will miss the God who longs to step in and transform their lives as well.

Discussion questions

1. Read Deuteronomy 1:26–40 and Numbers 14:31–33. What stopped the original generation rescued from Egypt from going into the Promised Land? What was the result? How did their lack of obedience affect the next generation?

2. In John 14:15 Jesus says, 'If you love me, you will obey what I command.' How important is obedience in the life of the Christian? Why?

3. What are the things that stop us from obeying God? What can we do about them?
4. What did God tell his people would be the impact of obedience? To what extent is the same true today? How evident is this in our modern world? Why?

3 The heart of the law

The law of the LORD is perfect,
reviving the soul.
The statutes of the LORD are trustworthy,
making wise the simple.
The precepts of the LORD are right,
giving joy to the heart.
The commands of the LORD are radiant,
giving light to the eyes.
(Psalm 19:7–8)

As we come to a book like Deuteronomy with a twenty-first-century mindset we find ourselves facing some difficulties. For one thing, so much has changed since those days on the plains of Moab. Culture, technology, lifestyle and communication have evolved to such an extent that most of us have little understanding of what life was like for the Israelites as they entered the Promised Land.

As well as these obvious physical changes, the impact of the life, death and resurrection of Jesus radically transformed our relationship to the law. While obedience to God's word remains a vital part of our relationship with him, there are fundamental differences in the position that we, by God's overwhelming grace, now find ourselves in.

If so much has changed, can we really learn anything from God's call to his people so long ago? It can be easy to forget that God, the unchanging one, remains the same. Contrary to what we sometimes subconsciously assume, he didn't undergo a transformation between Malachi and Matthew. God's intention and heart for his people are the same today as those outlined by Moses. The message of Deuteronomy, although written in a different time to a different set of people, is a message the people of God today desperately need to hear. Within its pages we can find principles for life that remain as unchanged by time and culture as the heart of God.

If we are in any doubt of the importance of God's law, we need only look at the life of Jesus. In fact, rather than sidelining or downgrading the law, Jesus said he came to fulfil it. In his life Jesus obeyed the law in a way that Israel had never been able to, demonstrating to the watching world what Torah looks like when it is lived from the heart. On one hand, through his death, Jesus replaced a covenant dependent on our obedience with one dependent on his. On the other, through his life, he showed us what our response to that gift should be.

I heard a story as a teenager that caused me to re-evaluate my attitude to God's law. A wealthy lady required a new chauffeur to transport her to and from her many engagements. Her palatial home was situated at the top of a cliff with magnificent views of the ocean. The problem was that the prime setting came with a catch. The only road to her home wound its way up the cliff face with numerous heart-stopping twists and bends. Without careful driving the occupants of the car could find themselves plunging into the ocean below. The lady decided to test the chauffeurs who applied for the job by asking them to drive her up the road to her house. The first was keen to show his driving skill. He attacked the road with great confidence, sometimes driving within a foot of the edge but still making it safely to the top. The second driver was even better. His depth perception and ability to judge speed enabled him to get within six inches of the edge while apparently completely in control. He reached the top smug and sure that the job was his. The third driver approached the road differently. Instead of showing how close he could safely get to the edge he tightly hugged the cliff face the whole way to the top. At the end of the process the job was given to the third driver. While the first two drivers heard only the restrictions, the third driver understood the purpose. Only he had understood that the aim was not to see how close you could get to the edge, but to use the road to help you safely navigate the treacherous terrain.

Although simplistic, this illustration highlights two different ways we can view God's law. It may seem unlikely that anyone would take such a foolish approach to a job interview and yet it is often the way we act towards God. The danger with laws that are set in stone is that we will try to observe them legalistically while nurturing hearts that are still in rebellion against God. We get as close to the edge as we can without technically crossing the line.

God says do not lie and so we learn to play around with words. We twist our sentences to achieve the desired result, but technically our words are true. God says do not commit adultery and so we do not have sex outside marriage. We may indulge in some 'harmless' flirtation or the odd fantasy, but physically we remain faithful. God says do not steal and so we take nothing without paying. We may browse the internet when we are being paid to work or find 'clever' ways to cut down our tax bill, but legally we are in the clear.

How close to the edge can you get? A foot? Six inches? Maybe at times you teeter right on the brink.

When we take this approach we misunderstand God's law completely and will never understand the book of Deuteronomy any more than we will understand the teachings of Jesus. We are like King Amaziah in 2 Chronicles 25:2 who 'did what was right in the eyes of the LORD, *but not whole-heartedly*' (my emphasis). The law was never meant as an obligation to be grudgingly fulfilled or a box to be ticked, but a road on which we can safely journey into the fullness of what God has for us. It is not about people whose behaviour is monitored, but a kingdom whose heart is changed. God does not want servants who submit out of duty, but sons who obey out of love.

Even if we see obedience to God as the response of a heart that wants to know him, parts of Deuteronomy present another problem. What do we do with the laws that seem so at odds with our culture? We understand the concepts of stealing and lying but how do you obey a law that no longer makes any cultural sense? Do you attempt to obey it as it stands or can it simply be set aside, no longer of any worth?

Let me give you an example of one such law. In Deuteronomy 22:8 the people are instructed that when they build a new house they are to make a parapet, or a protective rail, around the roof. You could attempt to obey this law by literally building a rail around the roof of your home. At best you may provide a new perch for the local bird life or at worst confirm to your neighbours that you are in fact odd, but you would indeed be following the letter of the law. This approach affirms the importance of the law but leads to the kind of burdensome legalism Jesus himself was so against.

The second way of dealing with this law is simply to discard it. Recognizing that, because of Jesus, you are no longer bound by the law, you could ignore it and presume it has no relevance to your life. While this approach embraces the freedom of the cross, it denies Jesus' confirmation of the law as God's design for life.

There is however a third approach. This is the approach which asks the question, what was the purpose of this law? Or to put it differently, what was God's heart for his people when he gave this law? In this case it is relatively easy, with a little digging, to uncover the intention behind the law. Unlike in rainy Northern Ireland, houses in Israel had flat roofs. Because of the way it was built the roof itself became an extra room used for cooking, as a playroom for children or for any other purpose common to daily life. Can you imagine the consequences if a flat roof was used constantly, with no protection against the drop to the ground below? The spirit behind this law was that the people of God were to have a practical concern for the lives of others. If they could take reasonable action to prevent someone else being harmed they were to do so.

Imagine the situation where, determined to obey the letter of the law, I painstakingly build a parapet around my roof. Job done, I get into my car and, anxious to get to my destination, I drive through my built-up neighbourhood at a speed of 45 mph. Have I obeyed Deuteronomy 22:8 to the letter? Yes. Have I understood the spirit of the law? Not at all! Despite my apparent religious observance I am putting at risk the lives of others and completely missing the point God was trying to teach his people.

God's intention is not that we become entrapped by legalistic attempts to slavishly fulfil the letter of the law. Instead, by looking at them from our vantage point of freedom in Christ, we begin to understand their purpose. As we discover more of his heart and allow his standards to govern all that we do, we become more like him. When we understand the life God always intended for the people who would reflect his holiness, we not only see the continuity with the New Testament, but we are better equipped to live our part in the story of his kingdom.

It is with this intention to search for God's heart for his people that we will look briefly at the life God lays before the Israelites in Deuteronomy, as he takes people who have been set free and begins to show them how to live in the good of their freedom. Rather than studying every law in detail, we will instead glean from them broad principles that will guide and shape our lives today, not as an intellectual exercise but as a practical attempt to better know the God we serve and to understand our role as his people.

Discussion questions

1. This chapter began with the words of Psalm 19:7–8. How does the psalmist view God's law? How does this compare to our view? Why?

2. In what ways is it possible to legalistically obey God's law, while at the same time missing its heart? How does that affect everyday life? How will it impact the people around us?

3. Read 2 Timothy 3:14–17. As Paul writes to Timothy, how does he describe the Scriptures? How will they eventually affect the man or woman of God? How do we know he is including the Old Testament?

4. If God has not changed, how will a grasp of Old Testament law help us grow in our understanding of (a) the heart of God, (b) New Testament teaching and (c) our place in the story?

4 Fear and freedom

The fear of the LORD is the beginning of wisdom.
(Proverbs 9:10 NASB)

The relationship the Israelites had with their God was inconceivable to those who watched from the outside. What a privilege to walk with God Almighty and enjoy his presence in their camp and his direction in their lives! With the passage of time, as Egypt faded into history and God's presence became an everyday reality, the Israelites began to face a danger that is all the more real today.

In the Disney movie *Aladdin*, one of the main characters is an oversized blue genie who bursts in technicolour from the end of a small brass lamp. By simply rubbing the lamp Aladdin can release the genie, who then uses his immense power to grant Aladdin his wish, even throwing in a cheerful song for good measure. Despite his phenomenal power the genie was confined to a tiny space and controlled by Aladdin's whims. One grave danger of our privileged relationship with God is that we will fall into the trap of viewing him like Aladdin's genie. Instead of an awesome God we see a pal who will turn up when we need some help, magically solving our problems or giving us a pick-me-up. If we are in trouble we schedule a prayer time and tell him what we need. Spiritually speaking, we rub the lamp and expect him to appear. Although God repeatedly cautions his people against this attitude, all too often the warning falls on deaf ears. When it does the consequences are disastrous.

We are in serious danger of losing sight of who God is, if we have not done so already. He is the creator of the universe, the all-powerful God, the one whose breath gave us life and without whom our hearts would cease to beat. He is the one to whom sin and rebellion were so abhorrent that he sent the children he loved from his presence to protect them from his wrath. Within the pages of Scripture we catch glimpses of a God whose splendour will take our breath away and whose holiness will drive us to our knees.

In C. S. Lewis' book, *The Lion, the Witch and the Wardrobe*, there is a moment when Susan and Lucy are talking to Mr and Mrs Badger about Aslan, the great king of Narnia. Having heard so many wonderful things about him, Susan is alarmed to hear that he is a lion and asks, 'Is he quite safe?' Mr Beaver's reply is interesting: 'Who said anything about safe? Course he isn't safe. But he's good. He's the king.'[1]

Our God is utterly good, but that goodness does not in any way diminish his all-consuming power. He cannot be limited and he cannot be controlled. In a world that has become comfortable in his presence we, like the children of Israel, would do well to remember that.

In Deuteronomy 5 Moses addresses this very problem. How is it possible to keep a correct view of God while at the same time enjoying an intimate relationship with him? It seems that the answer is by fearing him.

In today's world fear seems an unlikely basis for a deepening relationship. I think this is partly because we forget who God is, and partly because we often have a wrong understanding of what it means to fear him. To fear God is not simply to be frightened but to recognize the presence of the living God as a truly awesome place to stand. In order to remind the Israelites of the fear to which God calls them, Moses takes them back to Mount Sinai. When God appeared on Mount Sinai in fire and thunder the people were terrified. As the mountain shook, the voice of God struck into their hearts such terror that they expected to die. The fear consuming them was such that they were sure they could not survive another experience of God's presence and begged Moses, rather than God himself, to pass on the rest of the law.

God's response to their fear is a lesson we desperately need to learn. Rather than telling his people not to be afraid, he commended them on their response with these words, 'Oh that they had such a heart in them, that they would fear Me and keep all My commandments always, that it may be well with them and with their sons forever!' (Deuteronomy 5:29 NASB). It seems that God not only wanted his people to fear him but commanded them to do so. According to Deuteronomy 4:35 the awesome sights the Israelites witnessed were intended to show them that there was no-one like their God.

If the people of God were to walk with him and live as he intended, they must carry with them the same fear their parents felt at Sinai: fear that engraved on their hearts the holiness of God and reminded them that they had no right in themselves to stand in his presence; fear that is not just terror but also reverence, awe and respect; fear that puts God in his rightful place.

For a long time I found it difficult to understand how people called to live in fear of God could also know and love him. One day I was watching my husband playing with my eldest daughter, Ellie. The game was called monsters and the rules were simple. Glenn would roar, wave his arms menacingly and chase Ellie up the hall while she ran away screaming. The game continued for a while until Lara, who was about two at the time, wandered into the hall. Not wanting to leave her out Glenn turned, waved his arms menacingly and roared at her. The problem was that Lara had never played monsters and had no idea what was going on. For a moment she stood frozen to the spot, the colour draining from her face as her eyes opened like saucers. Then she did something I didn't expect. Instead of running away, she threw herself into Glenn's arms and buried her face in his chest. Why? Because she knew her father and she knew that, even when he seemed to be the source of her fear, the safest place to be was in his arms.

The people of Israel were not called to fear a strange God, they were called to revere a God they knew. This was not the paralysing fear of the unknown that attacked my fertile imagination as a child and drove me under my duvet every time I heard a creak or a groan. This was the awesome reverence of a God whose character they have seen and whose presence was their home. Interestingly, both their fear of God and their knowledge of him would come from the same place. Although they would experience his power in various ways, for this new generation and those to come, the fear of God would be born primarily out of the Word he had spoken. As they learned the laws of God and found in them his character, their awe of him would grow. Within his commandments they would discover the character of a God who was to be respected, a God whose power was all-consuming and yet whose heart was love. A God who was far above them and yet called them to walk with him. The presence of God would be right in their midst and yet his dwelling would be protected by laws so strict that they could not forget his holiness. The fear of God protected people with rebellious hearts from approaching their awesome God with anything less than reverent obedience.

Proverbs 9:10 also links wisdom to fearing God. If wisdom grows out of obedience to the word of God, and that obedience itself is a product of reverent fear, we can see why 'the fear of the LORD is the beginning of wisdom'. When we set aside our preconceived ideas of God and allow him to give us glimpses of who he really is, the result will be wholehearted obedience, which in turn produces the wisdom that comes only from him. Once again we are confronted with this very different view of wisdom. In the kingdom of God, true wisdom is the result of obedience, motivated by a heart in awe of a holy God.

There is another result of fearing God and it is one we often overlook. Rather than crippling the lives of the Israelites, the fear of God could bring them a freedom they had never known before. Alongside the commandment to fear God is a commandment to fear no-one else. When the Israelites had a correct understanding of the awesome power of God, it put into perspective the power of their enemies.

One of my favourite moments in *The Chronicles of Narnia* is in *Prince Caspian*, when the children have not just heard about Aslan but now know him personally. The film adaptation portrays the moment when, as battle rages around her, Lucy stands on a bridge with a tiny dagger in her hand. Coming towards her is an onslaught of enemies, who have the power to crush her in one blow. In the face of such opposition Lucy remains confident and unmoving. Why? Because behind her stands Aslan and in the face of his power the apparent might of all the opposing armies fades away to nothing.

When God's people have a proper understanding of who he is, their fear and awe of him will free them from fear of anything that shrinks in his presence. Daniel 6 tells the well-known story of a man so convinced of the power of his God that, even in the face of lions, he found the courage to stand firm. Centuries later Stephen, accused of following Jesus, faced the angry mob who stoned him to death, the name of his God still on his lips. What gave these men, and so many men and women like them, the courage to stand in the face of such terrifying circumstances? The God they knew filled them with such awe that nothing else could move them.

So often we refuse to see him as he is and settle instead for a lesser image of God. A manageable god created by society or tradition rather than the awesome God of the Bible, whose power and holiness are beyond anything our human minds can comprehend. When we, in our arrogance, presume to try to put him in a box for our personal use we discover that coming into the presence of our holy God without fear is a dangerous mistake indeed. Not only that, rather than finding courage in the fear of God, we will end up living lives that are crippled by the fear of things that we were never meant to try to conquer on our own.

Discussion questions

1. How is the fear of God different from fear as we commonly know it? What impact do the two kinds of fear have on our lives?

2. In what ways do we treat God like the genie in the lamp? In Leviticus 16:2 God makes it clear that Aaron, the High Priest, must not just come into the presence of God any way he chooses. Even he must live in reverent fear of God. Although Jesus made it possible for us to come freely into God's presence, what does this teach us about our attitude?

3. Read Acts 7. What was Stephen doing even as he faced his death? How did his understanding of the big story impact his faith in God? Why? What can we learn from this?

4. On what is your view of God based? Do you need to address this in any way? If so, how?

5 As for me and my house

*Sometimes the poorest man leaves his children
the richest inheritance.*
(Ruth E. Renkel)[1]

When the Israelites initially refused to go into the Promised
Land they not only forfeited the blessing God was longing to
give them, but also missed an opportunity to display to their
children the reality of their relationship with God. A generation who claimed to trust their God and believe his promises
showed by their behaviour that the opposite was true. If
actions speak louder than words, then all that they had spoken
was drowned out by the marching of their feet as they turned
and walked in the opposite direction.

Before this new generation of Israelites are commanded to
pass the law of God on to their children they are reminded of
the foundation on which this instruction is built. 'Hear O
Israel: The LORD our God, the LORD is one. Love the LORD
your God with all your heart and with all your soul and with
all your strength. These commandments that I give you today
are to be on your hearts' (Deuteronomy 6:4–6).

If the Israelites wanted to teach their children what it meant to live in relationship with God, it was vital that they demonstrated it in their own lives. Similarly, if we, as the people of God, want the next generation to witness the reality of God's presence, we must be collectively living in obedience to God's word ourselves. Each one of us has a part to play in shaping the next generation. Whether we have an active role in the life of children or play our part by modelling our obedience to God's word in the situation God has placed us, we have a responsibility to demonstrate openly the reality and authenticity of our faith in a trust-worthy God.

Moses knew that if the new generation of Israelites was to impress on their children the truth of God's word, they must first have wrestled with it for themselves, allowing it to sink deep into their hearts and become part of who they are. Rather than empty words, what they say must be an explanation for character and behaviour that is already evident in daily life. The mindset is not 'do as I say, not as I do' but 'take my hand and follow my lead'.

No-one sees through hypocrisy more quickly than children. I recently came home from a trip to the hairdressers and, pleased with myself, I asked my daughter what she thought of my new haircut. She studied me thoughtfully for a moment and then replied, 'Yes it's nice, but it's not about what you look like on the outside, it's about what's in your heart.' My initial laughter died on my lips as it occurred to me that, at the age of seven, she was analysing the truth of my words in the light of my behaviour. While I'm not suggesting for one moment that there is anything wrong with getting a new haircut, Ellie's words did make me stop and think for a moment about the messages we are sending the next generation.

If we tell them that the most important thing is the attitude of our hearts and then focus disproportionate amounts of time, energy and money on our appearance, do we really think they won't notice? If we say it is important to be kind to others and yet they hear us gossip with our friends, do we think they will turn a blind eye? If we tell our children they must show respect and then they watch as we speak harshly to those around us, what weight will our words carry? If we talk about the importance of God's word and yet spend every free moment glued to the television or computer, should we really be surprised when they don't believe us?

As they prepared to enter the Promised Land and live there as the people of God, Moses reminded the people that practical obedience to the law of God must first be lived out in the home. As clashing personalities, simmering tempers and bickering children were brought under the authority of his word, each new generation would grow to know God for themselves. If the law of God was to govern the nation, it must first govern families.

As we face the task of passing the word of God on to the next generation, there is perhaps nothing more challenging than living out our faith in the practical reality of family life. In an often hostile world the responsibility to guide and protect our children can become overwhelming. With this in mind, it is important to remember that the instructions in Deuter-onomy 6 were given to the nation of Israel as a whole and would have been understood within the context of the wider community. In the years that we have been parents, Glenn and I have been so grateful for the encouragement and support of other Christians, of various ages, who have become part of our family life. Whether it is a single musician from California, former missionaries with countless stories of the faithfulness of God or a young married couple who have intentionally committed to take an interest in the lives of our children, there are many people who have added to our daughters' lives in a way that we could not.

One group we particularly appreciate as parents are the students and young people we have come to know over the years. It is impossible to underestimate the impact of positive young role models for our children, particularly in a world where bad role models are so easy to come by. When our daughters see teens and young adults they look up to, who are prepared to take a stand and live for God, it powerfully reinforces the lessons we try to teach them on a daily basis and makes our job as parents so much easier.

As we attempt to raise our children, it is so important to remember that our responsibility is not to write their future but to teach them to know and trust the God who has a place for them in his story. As we mould and teach our children, the end product in our mind's eye must not be a picture we create, but the character of the God who created them in his image.

I remember as a child watching a man creating an ice sculpture of a swan. What began as a block of frozen water was slowly and steadily moulded, gradually changing shape until it became what the sculptor intended. To my untrained eye the chisel strokes seemed random but to him each one took the block of ice one step closer to becoming a swan. Just as the sculptor had in his mind's eye the sculpture he intended to create, the intention in teaching the law was to shape and nurture children so that they would grow to display the character of God.

Within the home the people are commanded to 'impress' the words of God upon their children. Just as the law was engraved on stone tablets to be preserved for future generations, the word of God was to be intentionally, permanently and clearly embedded in the hearts of the children. While we often assume that the best place to learn about God is in church, or perhaps a Bible study or even Bible college, the Israelites understood that the first place to discover the truth of God's word was in the home. It is easy to fall into the trap of believing that our children's understanding of the Bible is the responsibility of the church or of Sunday school teachers. However, if we as parents really believe that our children were created by God for a purpose that can only be found in him, then we are faced not only with the challenge of teaching them his word, but of cultivating homes which authentically demonstrate our own commitment to and reliance on it.

In a society that is driven by success and achievement, it is easy to spend so much time training our children for the future that we barely stop to consider the character they will have when they get there. Often we think nothing of early morning swim classes, weekend football, extra tutoring, dance class and music lessons, and yet we baulk at the idea of devoting time to studying the Bible. If we are to take this responsibility seriously, to 'bring them up in the training and instruction of the Lord' (Ephesians 6:4), what does it mean in practical terms?

For the Israelites, as for us today, the importance of this question cannot be overestimated and the answer is the heart of Deuteronomy 6. There is an important place for formally teaching our children to study the Bible. They need to learn to memorize it and understand it for themselves. If you are prepared to make time, there are an abundance of resources available for all ages and abilities that can help. It amazes me how often I hear adults claim that children cannot be expected to learn more than one or two short verses and yet those same children know the words to every song in the charts or the names of every player in the Premier League.

I have met countless people who desperately wish they had learned to study the Bible when they were young. As adults they know that the transformation God has brought about through his word in their later years would have revolutionized their early life. When we teach our children how to handle, understand and apply the word of God to their lives, we give them a gift that cannot be measured.

Having said that, I think Deuteronomy makes it clear that this commitment to God's word goes beyond formal teaching. In order to teach their children the word of God the Israelites are instructed to 'Talk about them when you sit and when you walk along the road, when you lie down and when you get up' (Deuteronomy 6:7). Does this mean every moment of every day has to be spent religiously studying the law? I don't think it does. Rather than excluding the rest of life, this command demonstrates the natural place God's word must have, permeating every aspect of life with its influence. Rather than seeing instruction in God's word as a regimented intrusion into an otherwise normal day, his presence should be like a perfume that leaves nothing untouched.

As we grow older, my brother and I are becoming more and more aware of the privilege we had as children. If you believe a home like the one described in Deuteronomy 6 would be joyless and dreary, I wish you could have grown up with my parents. While they have always been committed to God's word, very few of my childhood memories involve sitting at a table with a Bible in front of me. What I do remember clearly is the natural way God's presence seemed to fill our home. If I went into my parents' room at bedtime I would find them on their knees talking to the God who had governed their day. My dad's adventurous and infectious personality was, and still is, enhanced by his love for God rather than constrained by it.

One of my earliest memories took place on a walk with my dad when I was about five years old. We were walking, as we often did, along the sea wall near our home. Beyond the wall was a slope that went down to the water and dotted along it were several stone benches. I remember on that particular day a storm was gathering. The clouds were black and the sea was beginning to churn angrily. I remember my dad leading me down the slope to one of the benches where he sat down and tucked me inside his coat. There, with the salt air in our faces and the waves crashing below our feet he told me the story of Jonah. I have never forgotten that day or that story. Had he sat me down at home and read the story I have no doubt I would have learned something important. However, the impact of weaving the word of God spontaneously and naturally into everyday life has stayed with me for thirty years.

The difficulty with teaching children in this way is that it requires two things. Firstly, you have to spend time in God's word for yourself. If you have ever been in the position where you are expected to make an introduction to someone whose name you have forgotten, you will know how awkward it is. It is impossible to introduce our children to a God we do not know.

Secondly, you have to spend time with your children. It may seem obvious but if you are not with them you can't teach them. It may require cutting back on after-school activities, or working a little less overtime or even just turning off the television. Whatever it takes, can I encourage you to do it in the knowledge that the rewards infinitely outweigh the sacrifice and the result may last longer than you imagine?

Although my grandfather died when my mum was in her teens she remembers vividly the time she spent with him, as he allowed his love for God to overflow and colour his everyday life. She talks with great fondness of walks when he would point out trees and birds and speak with passion about the God who created them. He was not a rich man but his commitment to God and the influence it had on the next generation left a legacy that continues to impact our family fifty years after his death.

I write about my family cautiously and acutely aware that for many, many people this was not their experience. Even as I write I am deeply conscious that, despite the spiritual heritage I have, the gap between the parent I want to be and the parent I am is embarrassingly vast. We each come to God with our own past and our own present but, regardless of history, the responsibility to raise the next generation in the knowledge of God lies with us.

Rather than conforming to the drab religious stereotype, home as God intended is a place where his presence is a reality and the beauty of his character is lived out. Whether it is as you welcome friends to your table, walk down the street, give thanks for the food that sustains your body, learn to forgive one another or even deal with heartbreak, it is possible to use the ordinary moments to introduce your children to an extraordinary God.

When individuals, families and the wider community gave the word of God first place in their lives it not only offered the best protection from the dangers of the land they were about to enter, but would keep the Israelites from losing sight of who they were. As each generation grasped the importance of God's law, understood it correctly and lived it out, its place at the heart of their nation would be preserved. When children saw the reality of God in their home and in the lives of their parents and friends, they would ask why the commandments of God were so important. In response, one generation would have an opportunity to tell the next the story that changed their lives. As the story was passed on a new generation would see and believe that to fear the Lord and obey his statutes was not only for their survival but for their very best.

Discussion questions

1. In Colossians 3:17, Paul reminds the believers that every aspect of life should reflect the presence of Jesus. How does this reinforce God's instructions regarding the home?
2. What is the difference between teaching children to display the character of God and moulding them to be the person we want them to be? How is their freedom and individuality impacted by each? How is God's sovereignty in their lives impacted by each?
3. Read Judges 2:10. What are the dangers of failing to pass God's word on to our children? In what way is this already evident in the world around us?
4. If you are a parent, what can you do to help your children grow in their understanding of God's word? How could other Christians, perhaps from different stages of life, help in this task?

6 The danger from outside

Seducers are more dangerous enemies
to the church than persecutors.
(Matthew Henry)[1]

During my third year at university I fulfilled an ambition I have had since I was a little girl. I became a published poet. Let me tell you the story.

One day I read an article which caught my interest. A new anthology of poetry was to be compiled and the editors were looking for previously unpublished poets whose work could be considered for inclusion in the book. Thinking I had nothing to lose, I selected what I felt was my best poem and sent it off. A few weeks later I got a letter telling me that I had reached the next stage in the selection process. As you can imagine, I began to get quite excited. As I continued to get closer to the final stage of selection my anticipation grew, until at last I got a letter confirming that my work had been chosen.

After sending off my £35 contribution and agreeing to release my poem for publication the wait seemed endless. Finally the day arrived. I could barely contain myself until the postman left and I tore off the packaging. As I opened the enormous book I became uneasy. By the time I had turned a few pages I was beginning to feel ill. As promised, my poem had been published. I suspect the same was true of every other poem which had been submitted. The book in which I featured was not a selective celebration of literary talent but a money-making racket. I was not chosen because I was gifted, but because I was gullible.

Do you know what the worst part was? No-one broke into my house and stole my work. No-one hacked into my computer and plagiarized my poem. I printed it. I put it in an envelope and I sent it to them. Not only that, I paid for the privilege.

As the Israelites prepared to enter their new home they faced a very real danger. Although the nations who currently possessed the land were larger and stronger, they had no power to take what God had given his people. Their enemies were powerless against an awesome God. If Israel walked with him, the danger was not that they would be defeated in battle; the danger was that the Israelites would willingly give up the blessings of their inheritance – because they had been taken in by people who promised much but delivered nothing. That they, like me, would be left with no-one to blame but themselves.

In order to protect them from their own capacity to be drawn away, God gave his people very clear instructions regarding the people who already occupied the land. Once God had defeated their enemies and given Israel the land, they were to utterly destroy the nations who were living there. They were not to make covenants with them or show them favour. They were not to marry them or allow their children to marry them.

If I'm honest, there is still a part of me that shrinks back from the ruthlessness to which God called the Israelites. I was part of a group studying Joshua recently and when we came to Joshua 10 and 11, where these commands are obeyed and the destruction is total, most people readily admitted that they had found the passages very difficult to understand. This is the side of God that many of us struggle with most. How could a loving God order his people to wipe out entire nations?

People whose knowledge and debating skill is far greater than my own have argued this point for generations. A few have used it as license to commit all sorts of atrocities in God's name. Others have found fodder for their attack against the Christian faith, pointing to a God who is brutal and untrustworthy.

As I try to wrap my head around this issue I have found it helpful to remember that, as history unfolded, there was always a bigger picture. What God sees is not what I see. If he were limited by my mental capacity the world would be a very small place indeed. There comes a point when I have to accept that there are things I will never fully understand. It is my responsibility, with the help of the Holy Spirit, to study and intelligently think through the truth I find in Scripture. However, when I, in my arrogance, demand that a holy God explains himself to me fully, I am on dangerous ground.

When you take a step back and look at the span of the Bible, things look a little different. The nations occupying the land were not innocent bystanders encountering God for the first time. They were not simply in the wrong place at the wrong time. The societies and practices of the surrounding nations would make some of the darkest films of modern times pale in comparison. In Genesis 15:16 God speaks to Abraham about the Amorites, one of the nations the Israelites were commanded to destroy. He shows Abraham that it was not until the Amorites had reached the point of no return, when their brutality and evil was complete, that God would destroy them. In Genesis 18 Abraham discovered that God was going to destroy the evil cities of Sodom and Gomorrah. Knowing that God was just, Abraham asked him to spare the cities if they could find even ten people who were righteous. Other than Lot, who by our standards seems an unlikely candidate, there were none. Even Lot and his family had to be dragged reluctantly from the city that would have destroyed them.

I have often found that the very people who struggle most with passages like this are the first to condemn God for not stepping in to wipe out the evil in our world. Pointing their finger at God they ask why people like Hitler, bin Laden and others have been allowed to inflict pain and suffering on countless innocent people. God's response to sin and evil in the Old Testament is both a promise and a caution.

The promise is that evil, which seems to saturate the world, does not go unseen. Neither will it be allowed to continue forever. Just as the Hitlers and bin Ladens of this world will answer for their actions, the abusive, the violent, the gossips, the greedy and the people who break the hearts of those entrusted to their care will find that they can't fool God.

Which brings us to the caution. It seems that in a world where people are free to make whatever choices they want without condemnation, where consequence often takes a back seat to rights, there have never been more people in more pain. The truth is that we have gone after the wrong kind of freedom. True freedom is not the freedom to do whatever we want but the freedom to be the people we were meant to be. To think we can do anything we please and be happy is a lie that our culture has sold us on so many levels. When we demand our right to make our own choices, however selfish, we also have to accept that those choices will have consequences.

The God who had walked with the Israelites and knew their hearts could see what a life steeped in the idolatry of these nations led to. In Deuteronomy 7 he reminds them again why they have been set free. They are free to be a holy people. A nation chosen to walk with him and reflect his heart to a world he loves. He reminds them again of his faithfulness and of the blessings that he will pour upon them if they keep his commandments and do not allow themselves to be drawn away from him.

Do you remember the tender-hearted surgeon? The father whose understanding of the danger caused him to cut into the body of his son, not to wound him, but to stop the cancer that would ultimately take his life? If imperfect people like you and I struggle with the destruction of the other nations, how can we begin to imagine that it did not tear at the heart of God? This is the God who chose Israel to be his people, through them continuing to pursue a world which had forgotten who he was. This is the God who was prepared to reduce himself into the body of a man and eventually die a brutal and excruciating death to rescue the world he loves. Rather than being tempted to doubt the heart of the God we know, we should consider the gravity of a danger that would cause a God of love to take such drastic action.

The idolatry that characterized these nations was a road to nowhere and God knew it. He also knew that, unless the Israelites were determined and ruthless in avoiding idolatry, they would quickly succumb to the temptations all around them. As they began to work their land they would look over the fence at their Canaanite neighbour's field. Perhaps they would ask him why his land was so lush. When they discovered that he offered sacrifices to Baal a seed of doubt would be planted. Was obedience really enough? Would God really give them all they needed if they simply did as he asked?

Perhaps they should use their own initiative and learn from their neighbours? Maybe one sacrifice to Baal just to make sure? And so it would begin.

Men who had wandered in the desert for forty years would look at the colourful women of Canaan and be drawn to them like insects to the light. Surely, if they married them, then the Canaanite women would eventually worship the God of Israel? Instead the women brought idols into their homes. To keep the peace, their husbands said nothing. As the children grew, instead of learning about the God of Israel they were taught about the gods of their mothers and the ways they could be pleased. And so it began.

The God who sees the future as clearly as he sees the present and the heart as clearly as the action understood that the Israelites would not hold fast. Like me, eager to become a published poet, they would see something they really wanted and fall for the lies they were told. They would willingly give what could never be stolen. Because he understood what was at stake for the Israelites, and ultimately for mankind, he knew that the idolatrous nations had to go.

God's instructions to wipe out other nations were specific to that time and place and must not be taken as a general rule. They do not give anyone licence to behave in any way that is contrary to the compassionate heart of God. Commands such as these were given to Israel as part of their calling to establish a physical nation. In contrast, as the people of God today we find ourselves spread throughout the world, charged with living out the love of God until such times as Jesus returns. In Matthew 5, Jesus makes it clear that to follow him means loving even those who would be considered enemies, going the extra mile and repaying evil with good. In the parable of the good Samaritan (Luke 10:25–37) Jesus shows that love, in the kingdom of God, is not constrained by cultural or racial barriers. It is worth noting that, even in Deuteronomy, the intention or spirit behind these laws was not destruction but protection of the holiness that is always central to God's plan for his people. With this in mind, if we are to live the lives we are called to, enjoying the presence of a holy God, we must understand how easily we can be drawn into idolatry of our own.

A few years ago I was working on my computer and my husband, Glenn, was going out to play football. I looked up briefly as he said goodbye but it wasn't until a few minutes later, when it was too late to warn him, that I realized something was wrong with his football kit. The previous day he had decided to wash his shorts and so, as they were white, he did some of the other white washing at the same time. The problem was that Glenn is colour blind. For most people the pink top in the middle of the pile would have been immediately visible, but to Glenn it looked as white as the rest of the washing. Which was why, as he headed out to football, he was now wearing pink shorts.

All too often we turn a blind eye to the things we do that make us stumble in our walk with God. It is easy to see a wooden idol or a stone god. The idolatry that tends to grip our hearts and draw us away from him is much more difficult to spot. An idol is simply anything that is put in the place where God should be and the warnings against it are as clear in the New Testament as they are in the Old. So deadly is the danger that in 1 Corinthians 10:14, as he reminds them of the lessons they must learn from the life of the early Israelites, the apostle Paul urges the church not just to be careful but to *flee* from idolatry.

From our earliest moments each of us has the capacity to create for ourselves idols of every kind imaginable. We make idols of popularity and beauty and fame and sport and money and career and anything and everything we can find. We can take the greatest blessings that God has given us and twist and mould them until they become the very things that keep us from God. If we are to protect ourselves from this danger, which so offended the heart of a holy God, we must be ruthless about the things that captivate our minds. For the Israelites, protection from idolatry came from obedience to the commands of God. For us it is no different.

My husband's difficulties with the washing arose because he could not see the pink top that coloured everything it touched. Unless we are people of God's word, allowing our thoughts and attitudes to be intentionally shaped by his character, we will be blind to the things that will be our downfall. When that happens the consequences will be infinitely more serious than the mocking Glenn received on the football field.

By allowing our minds to be shaped by the culture around us we forfeit so much that could have been ours. We destroy our relationship with God and our effectiveness in the task he has called us to. We may be blind to the things that we put before God. He is not. When the Israelites' obedience was half-hearted they learned that they were easily defeated. In contrast, when they put God's commands into practice, the victories they saw were astonishing.

Your idols and mine may be different. The impact they have is the same. When we allow ourselves to be driven by gods of our own making we open our hands and give up what can never be taken from us. Not only that, we pay for the privilege.

Discussion questions

1. In modern life, what are some of the things which commonly threaten to derail us in our walk with God? How easy is it to identify the things that pose the greatest danger to us as individuals? Why?

2. How could God's word protect the Israelites from being drawn away from him? Read John 17:15–17 where Jesus prays for his disciples. What role does God's word play in protecting us today?

3. What is an idol? Why does God take idolatry so seriously? How will it affect us?

4. If we can be so easily distracted and drawn away from God, are there any practical steps we can take to control the things that influence us?

7 Living with blessing

*In appreciation of beauty, mountains, music, poetry,
knowledge, people, science – even in the tang of an apple –
God is there, to reflect the joy of his presence in the believer
who will realise God's purpose in all things.*
(Pete Fleming, martyr in Ecuador)[1]

Like most people, I can look back at times when life seemed
very dark. There have been days when I have sat on the floor
and cried as I clung to the God whose presence was the only
calm in the storm that seemed to rage around me. I have
discovered that, for me, these are not the dangerous times.
In my life the greatest threat comes in the times when the
sky is cloudless and blessing casts a warm glow on the path
ahead.

On days like that my wandering heart begins to celebrate
the things that I have done. As I contemplate my successes
and pat my own back I am less likely to throw myself on God.
My desire for him begins to cool and my hold on him weakens.
I am king of all I survey and God has been dethroned. That
is when I find myself in the greatest danger.

As they entered their inheritance the Israelites faced a battle on two fronts. One was the danger of becoming caught up in the idolatry of those around them, making anything but God the greatest desire of their heart. The other was closer to home. As they walked into the Promised Land and left the desert years behind, the Israelites would find themselves in a land whose beauty and abundance stood in contrast to all they had known. People who had lived on manna would feast instead on wheat and barley and marvel at the tastes of figs, olives, honey and pomegranates. Instead of water from a rock they would stand under waterfalls of cool clean water and drink until they could drink no more. With full bellies and thirst that was finally quenched they would work land bursting with iron and copper. At night, as they laid their heads down in their own homes and listened to the satisfied breathing of their children, they would find that they lacked nothing. It was in those moments of contentment and physical security that the danger, as subtle as it was deadly, would creep into their hearts.

Deuteronomy 8 gives the people a unique window into some of the lessons God had been teaching them in the desert. The forty years of wandering that began because of their own rebellion were turned by God into an opportunity to grow. An opportunity to prepare themselves for a future that only God could see.

In the desert God let his people experience hunger so that they would discover the manna that came only from him. During those years the Israelites learned that God was the one who sustained them. The food that satisfied their hunger was not the result of their own labour. It came directly from the hand of God. As they paused before each meal to give thanks it was not a religious ritual, but recognition of the fact that they were utterly dependent on him. In words later quoted by Jesus himself, Deuteronomy 8:3 reminds the Israelites that 'man does not live on bread alone, but on every word that comes out of the mouth of the LORD'. The people discovered that, while the food they ate sustained their bodies, only God could give them life.

The land God led his people into was a good land. The blessings showered upon them were to be enjoyed and celebrated. To enter into the blessing of Canaan and continue to live as though they were in the desert would have been an affront to the generosity of their God.

I have a friend whose Bible teaching has profoundly affected my own life. He is one of those people whose knowledge of and passion for God's word is utterly contagious. I remember hearing him speak once about God's desire that we would enjoy the world he has made. He described in detail the moment when you first bite into a piece of hot, steaming battered fish. Perhaps it may seem an odd illustration to choose, yet the twinkle in his eye was unmistakable. The result of a lifetime devoted to understanding and teaching the Scriptures was a deep delight in God that served only to increase his appreciation of even the simplest blessings.

This is the attitude to which God called the Israelites. Not to deny his goodness but to recognize the source of their blessing. To return their thanks to him with the joy of a child who has received a gift which exceeded all their expectations.

In the midst of so much promise Moses gives the people a warning. As they build houses and live in them and watch their cattle multiply and their wealth increase, they are not to let pride creep in. A nation taken out of slavery by their powerful God was to fight the temptation to congratulate themselves on their achievements. Even in blessing, they are called to remember the lessons of the desert. To live in the knowledge that everything they have is a gift from the hand of God.

There is a wonderful chapter in the book *Sitting at the Feet of Rabbi Jesus* which explains the Jewish practice of *berakhah*. These countless one line prayers of thanksgiving to God were woven into the fabric of life, training the hearts of the people to acknowledge God's goodness in all things. As the writers explain,

> You bless God when you see the ocean for the first time in a long while or a king in his royal procession. You bless him if you see an exceptionally beautiful person or a gifted rabbi. You utter a word of praise if you are reunited with a long-lost friend. When you peel a fresh orange and whiff its bracing, zingy scent, you praise God, saying, 'Blessed is he who has given a pleasant smell to fruits.'[2]

What a powerful way to cultivate an awareness of their dependence on God! Even in their waking moments they would begin with a simple prayer of thanksgiving to God for returning their soul to them for another day. Such a constant attitude of praise is a fitting response to the warnings God gave his people in Deuteronomy 8. When they have eaten and are satisfied, they are to bless the Lord for all that he has given them and to be careful that they do not forget their God.

What does it mean to forget God? When we hear those words today we understand them to mean that the thought of God has slipped from the minds of the people. However, in this context, forgetting is more than a mental lapse. In biblical Hebrew to remember is associated with taking action. In Genesis 40:14, when Joseph urges the cupbearer to 'remember' him, he is not asking to be thought of fondly, he wants the butler to take action to help him get out of prison. In Exodus 2:24, when it says that God 'remembered' his covenant with Abraham, Isaac and Jacob, it means that he took action and rescued his people. To remember God is to obey him, to continue to walk in his ways and follow his laws. For God's people, to forget him did not just mean they stopped thinking about him, but that they no longer gave him first place.

To say that we have forgotten God does not just mean we can't remember. It means we no longer behave as though God has any authority in our lives. Rather than seeing life as a gift from him we delude ourselves into believing we are in control of our own happiness. We accept that wealth and achievement will bring joy, even though the most profound emptiness is often found in those who seem to have everything.

Close to my grandfather's grave is a headstone that caught my attention as a child. Buried there is Ludwig Schenkel, an Austrian Jew who settled in Londonderry after the Second World War. He was a skilled photographer whose captivating images of the surrounding area were displayed in magazines and exhibitions. The thing that struck me about Ludwig Schenkel was the message he chose to leave for the world. A man whose skills brought him success and whose eyes were tuned to beauty chose this epitaph: 'And all the dreams I ever dreamt came to nothing, nothing meant.'

King Solomon was one of the richest men who ever lived, enjoying wealth, abundance and power on a scale most people can't begin to comprehend. He denied himself nothing. Yet, after he had filled his life with every conceivable pleasure, he came to this conclusion: 'When I surveyed all that my hands had done and what I toiled to achieve, everything was meaningless, a chasing after the wind' (Ecclesiastes 2:11).

Rather than causing him to worship God, Solomon's great wealth drew him farther and farther from his creator. The farther he got from God, the farther he got from all he was created to be.

God knew the dangers for Israel. He knew that the very blessings he showered on them could draw them away from him and so he put in place provisions to help them remember. By now, you will not be surprised to hear that the first thing to keep the Israelites from settling for these blessings and missing life was their commitment to the law their God had given them. He understood that prosperity in itself was not a dream that would satisfy but a responsibility that could destroy them if they tried to carry it alone.

God also put into place specific times for the people of Israel to come before him together and rejoice in all that he had done. Not to dress in sackcloth and ashes or deny what God had given them. Not to sombrely denounce their blessings, but to stand with overflowing hearts in the presence of the God who invented joy. The offerings God asked them to bring were not given in payment or as an attempt to secure his favour. Instead they were bringing to God a physical token of their heartfelt thanks for the blessings he had poured into their lives. The offerings they brought were a continual reminder that what they had came from him.

Can you imagine the first time they stood before God in this way, as the smell of freshly dug earth filled the air and the colours and sounds of harvest thrilled their senses? The produce of their own land, given to them by God, was finally in their hands. Do you think their offerings were grudging or their worship forced? I don't know if they danced but I imagine they may have. I think I would have. By nature I am a reserved person. My lack of coordination meant I bore the brunt of family jokes as a child and if ever an occasion calls for dancing I will usually be found holding the coats! However, if you had been walking along a deserted country road in the Cotswolds on an unremarkable Thursday afternoon in 2005 you may have seen me dance. The reason was simple. During the week that had passed, God had answered prayers I had only prayed in the very deepest parts of my heart. Prayers that no-one knew about but me. Confronted with the indescribable goodness of God I found myself so overwhelmed with joy that I forgot my reservations and danced with the joy of being his.

I think this is the joy God wanted his people to have when they came together to remember his goodness. The explosive joy that sets your heart on fire and is the antidote to the temptation to settle for anything less than him.

When the everyday work of cultivating the ground, feeding families and breeding cattle began to eat away at this joy and the reality of God's goodness threatened to be lost in the hum of commerce, another feast would come around. Another holy-day designed to help God's people intentionally remember his goodness. Another time to come together as a nation and pour out their thanks to the God who had given them so much.

What if, when we came together as his people, we came with hearts that had that same degree of thankfulness? What if we allowed God to show us, as if for the first time, the blessings that he has poured into our lives? What if, whatever our circumstances, we really understood what it means to be rich?

The spiritual riches of life in Christ are the inheritance of every child of God. Physical riches, on the other hand, are not ours by right. They are not an indication that we have earned special favour with God, nor will they in themselves ever bring the satisfaction that our souls crave. You may not consider yourself wealthy, but if you have food in your fridge, clothes on your back and enough money to buy this book then, compared to the majority of the world's population, you are rich. Don't be fooled into thinking that what you have is yours by right. Financial prosperity comes with great danger as well as great responsibility. If you do find yourself living a life of relative abundance, beware of believing you are building an empire with your own two hands. When you allow yourself to believe that you are the author of your own happiness, the story you write for yourself will be small indeed.

When we intentionally allow God to train us to see what we have in him, we are reminded where blessing comes from in the first place. By committing ourselves to his word and to coming into his presence individually and corporately to worship, we do what Ludwig Schenkel and King Solomon failed to do. We enjoy God's blessings and we use them in every way we can to bring him glory, but we set our hearts on a bigger dream.

If for now the sun is shining in your life, don't live like you are standing in the rain. Delight in God's blessings whatever form they take and allow them to multiply in your heart the joy that can be found in life. If God has entrusted you with financial wealth, remember where it comes from and use it accordingly. If you have skills or talents, work hard at them. Make them as good as they can be and bring them first to God with the thankfulness of a heart that knows they came from him. If God has placed within you a passion for cooking or surfing or medicine or music or nature or farming, or anything else that reflects the image of the God who created you, enjoy it. Just make sure you do it from the overflow of a heart that first finds its satisfaction in God and recognizes that the source of every blessing is him alone.

We are not the kings of all we survey. We are the children of a generous Father whose riches are greater and more abundant than anything we could build with our own two hands. When we dethrone God we trade in the big dreams he has for us and replace them with the little ones we create for ourselves. God's heart for us is so much more than physical blessings or financial wealth. His desire is that we learn to live life to the full, delighting in the riches that can be found in abundance or famine by the heart that is already satisfied in him.

Discussion questions

1. What are the dangers and responsibilities that come with financial prosperity?
2. Read Philippians 4:11–13. How do Paul's physical circumstances affect his relationship with God? What is the secret of his contentment?
3. Read Matthew 6:19–21. According to Jesus, what is the difference between treasures on earth and treasures in heaven? How does our attitude to wealth affect our heart?
4. According to Ephesians 1:3, God has 'blessed us in the heavenly realms with every spiritual blessing in Christ'. How would a deep awareness of this truth impact our approach to physical blessing? What practical steps can we take to continually remind ourselves of this reality?

8 The call to holiness

It's so easy to cash in these chips on my shoulder,
So easy to loose this old tongue like a tiger,
It's easy to let all this bitterness smoulder
Just to hide it away like a cigarette lighter.
It's easy to curse and to hurt and to hinder,
It's easy to not have the heart to remember
That I am a priest and a prince in the kingdom of God.
(Andrew Peterson, 'Fool with a fancy guitar')[1]

What does holiness mean to you? If someone you had never met was described as holy, how would you picture them in your mind? Would you look for someone carrying a large Bible, sniffing disdainfully every time they caught the slightest hint of fun? Would you expect them to keep their distance for fear of contamination by the likes of you? Perhaps you would feel the need to perform in their presence, to be someone other than who you really are?

So many of us, perhaps even subconsciously, have grown up with this view of holiness. If holiness is opposed to freedom and joy then our lack of holy desire is hardly surprising. But what if we have got it wrong? What if the view of holiness we have settled for is nothing more than a caricature conjured up in our own imaginations?

From the very beginning holiness has been the calling of the people of God. As the Israelites prepare to enter the Promised Land they are reminded again, in Deuteronomy 14:2, what it is they are called to be: 'For you are a people holy to the Lord your God. Out of all the peoples on the face of the earth, the Lord has chosen you to be his treasured possession.' Within his law the Israelites have already encountered a God who delights to bless his people and fill their lives with purpose and joy. If this same God calls them to be marked out by holiness then it has to be something very different from the common perception. If holiness is the stamp by which they are identified as his, what does it look like?

The book of Leviticus is saturated with the holiness of God and his requirements for the people who are called to walk with him. Nestled within its pages is the secret to understanding what holiness is. When God says 'Be holy, for I am holy' (Leviticus 11:45), he not only tells his people why they are to be holy, he tells them what holiness is. Rather than a list of standards they must abide by, the holiness God calls his people to is a reflection of his character. God does not just do holy things, he *is* holy. Holiness is his very essence and, as his people, the Israelites were called to reflect and display that essence to the world.

This calling left the Israelites with an apparent dilemma. How could a nation whose hearts were inherently rebellious even begin to display the character of God? Could a rag-tag bunch of travellers really become a holy nation? Until the Israelites understood who he was, they could never understand what it meant to be like him. If the law was the place where God's people could uncover his heart, where they could learn who he was and who he wanted them to be, then it was where holiness began. It started with people who were committed to their God and to the calling he had given them. With people who were determined, whatever the cost, to let their minds be shaped and directed first by God himself. It started in the quiet places, in the morning stillness as another day began with the words of God. In the moments when families gathered to hear the Scriptures read. In the memorizing of the law as it continued to shape and fashion the heart of a nation until it beat in time with the heart of God. However, while holiness began in the quiet places, it did not end there.

For the people of God, holiness was never intended to be about theory. It was not an ethereal quality that hovered over the spiritually smug. It was never something to be simply studied or meditated upon or even debated. It was something to be lived. Holiness that shows itself only in the quiet places is not holiness at all.

One of the most striking things about the book of Deuteronomy is God's involvement in the intimate details of everyday life. Oswald Chambers put it this way: 'When a man says he must develop a holy life alone with God, he is of no more use to his fellow men; he puts himself on a pedestal, away from the common run of men.'[2] The holiness of God did not withdraw from life, it transformed it. God's character is best seen not in the recluse who withdraws from the world in an attempt to purify himself, but in the carpenter with the calloused hands and dusty feet who was so different and yet so irresistible, even to those society had cast aside.

If the law of God stood apart from that of the surrounding nations, then God's people, as they lived out his law, would also be different. Different in the way they conducted business. Different in the way they ran their homes. Different in the way they treated slaves. Different in the way they cared for the world around them. Different in the way they approached battle. Different in the way they fought for justice. Different in the way they worshipped their God. In those differences the holiness of God would shine.

When we begin to understand that holiness for the Israelites was a reflection of the God who called them his, we come up against a problem that makes many twenty-first-century Christians uncomfortable. If we are content with the misconception that holiness earned the Israelites their place with God we can study books like Deuteronomy unmoved. We are told constantly, and quite rightly, that we can be accepted by God only on the basis of what Jesus did on the cross. We can never, even through a lifetime of trying, earn a place in God's kingdom. God accepts us as we are. To understand that truth is to understand freedom, but it is not the end of the story. We have become so determined to emphasize our freedom that we forget why it was given.

If Israel's holiness was an expression of the character of a God who had already accepted them then we, although secure in our relationship with God, face the same call. While holiness cannot earn you a place in God's kingdom it is the evidence that his kingdom is present. If the Israelites were called to be a 'people holy to the LORD', showing by their lives that they belonged to him, how does that calling relate to me?

After the death and resurrection of Jesus, Peter wrote to the church which had been scattered because of persecution, encouraging and instructing them as they lived as God's people in a hostile world. In 1 Peter 2:9, as he urged them to live out their calling he wrote, 'You are a chosen people, a royal priesthood, a holy nation, a people belonging to God, that you may declare the praises of him who called you out of darkness into his wonderful light.' Quoting Deuteronomy,

Peter shows the church that their call to holiness is the same. As God's people they are to reflect his character in their daily lives, showing the world around them the beauty of the God to whom they belong. To be holy as he is holy.

When Jesus came he did not eliminate the need for holiness. He came because without him holiness was impossible. He did not come to lower the bar, but to raise it and then make it possible for us to reach.

I sat at a table recently with two Christian women as they talked about their teenage children. Their concern was deep and genuine as they struggled to raise their families in a world already so different from the one they grew up in. I was struck by a comment one of them made. She said, 'It used to be that there was a clear line between what Christians do and don't do. That line seems to be gone now. I blame my generation for that.' She went on to say that she believed many of her generation had responded to the joyless legalism they grew up with by embracing what they thought was freedom and behaving as they pleased. As they dealt with the difficulties their children now faced, the pressure to conform and the lack of boundaries, it became obvious that this apparent freedom had left their children lost and confused rather than liberated.

While we have already established that God's plan for his people was never religious drudgery, freedom is not the absence of standards. Just as the Israelites were called to live God's character, we too are called to be different. Different in how we treat people. Different in how we conduct business. Different in how we care for the world around us. Different in how we treat money. Different in our relationships. As Christians today, how different are we?

As a person with a rebellious heart of my own, how do I start to become more like a holy God? Just like the Israelites I need to understand who he is. Like them, I need to allow his heartbeat to change the rhythm of my own. If holiness is a reflection of the character of God then it is not something that is manufactured, but cultivated. If I want to live an everyday life infused with the holiness of God, I must begin by getting to know him and intentionally bringing my life under his authority.

I have a friend who moved to Italy some years ago. At first she found the language difficult, constantly thinking in English and translating every sentence in her head. After some time she found herself thinking in Italian. I remember her excitement as, after a considerable time, she told me she had dreamt in Italian. Gradually the language she surrounded herself with and studied became part of her until eventually she used it without conscious thought.

The same is true of us. We will never become like God without spending time in his presence. It is so easy to become people who have time for anything but him. We buy into the lie that television is relaxing but time with God is work. We cling to that extra half hour in bed, believing it will give us more strength than half an hour in the presence of the one who gives us breath. We even serve him, running from place to place until there is no time left to know him. Again and again we settle for what we are instead of what we could be. Yet, when we overrule our natural instincts and choose to please God instead, he begins to do things that will take our breath away.

As God's people we are sorely in need of an experience like the one the Israelites had in Nehemiah 8. In the centuries following their possession of the Promised Land, the nation of Israel had drifted far from the standards God had given them. Despite God's warnings and his attempts to draw them back to himself, they had rebelled and squandered all that he had given until eventually they ended up in exile. Nehemiah vividly describes the events which took place years later, when some of the Israelites were able to return to their land. Faced with past failure, the nation of Israel gathered to hear the law that God had given through Moses so many years before. In reverent silence they listened as the word of God was explained to them. Overwhelmed by their own disobedience and confronted by all they should have been, the people of God began to weep. Yet, in their grief, they discovered that there was a way back. Can you imagine the joy that rippled through the crowd as they began to realize there was still hope? Even for a people who had failed again and again, an encounter with the holy God turned their weeping into celebration.

I witnessed the reality of this transformation recently in the life of a young woman called Lucy. In her late teens Lucy decided to embrace what she thought was freedom, throwing herself into a lifestyle with no restraints. When I met her again as a young adult she was deeply unhappy, torn between the memories of a God who loved her and a lifestyle she didn't want to lose. As she read God's word, Lucy knew that giving her life to God would mean making some painful choices. When she finally gave up the struggle and allowed God to take control, the change was incredible. Despite the tough changes Lucy was facing in her life, her beaming face told the story of a joy she had almost given up on having. In the presence of God she discovered that to pursue holiness is to find freedom.

If we want to live our part in God's story, to discover what we were created for, we can only do that by returning to his word. It may be that we will find ourselves faced with things we would rather ignore. It may be that we are moved to tears by the reality of our own disobedience. However, as the Israelites did, we will find that God's word always offers hope. If we want to know what it means to live as the people of

God, the only way to do it is to immerse ourselves in his word, placing our lives under its authority and allowing it to be the voice that guides us. Only then will it become the standard by which we live.

As a child I grew up in a church where most people chose not to own a television. I remember hearing about a man who decided he would buy one and had it delivered to his house. When it arrived he saw emblazoned on the side of the box the words 'Bringing the world into your home'. He took one look at the slogan and returned the television, informing the delivery driver that he would not be bringing the world into his home. I used to laugh at that story but, as I get older, I wonder if he was more astute than I realized. I'm not suggesting we all get rid of our televisions. But we do need to give serious thought to both the quality and the quantity of the programmes we are watching. In today's world there are so many things that can provide us with instant distraction. Whether it is television or surfing the internet, video games or smartphones, it is so easy to fill our minds with things that at best give us no benefit and at worst draw us further and further from God. If we are going to live as God intended, we have to be conscious of what is shaping our lives and, when it is the wrong things, we need to be ruthless. As a generation we have become so comfortable with our culture that we barely feel it chip away at the image of God in our lives, until, instead of his holiness, we end up reflecting nothing more than the world we live in.

My husband spends a large amount of time in our local schools, speaking to children and young people of all ages, often with opportunities to share stories from the Bible. One day as he walked along the street a little boy stopped and tugged on his mother's coat. As he passed, Glenn heard the boy whisper, 'Mummy, there's God!'

We are the people of an awesome God and, whether we realize it or not, we are representing him. If we are the princes and priests in the kingdom of God then we have a responsibility to represent him correctly. Not by retreating into our own little community but by intentionally cultivating the character of God so that when we go out into the playgrounds, supermarkets, offices, boardrooms and homes of our world we will take with us evidence of who God really is. Paul, in Titus 2:10, describes it as adorning the doctrine of God (NASB). In other words, taking God's word and putting flesh on it in a way that shows its beauty to a watching world. Unlike the Israelites, we not only have the example of Jesus to follow, but the presence of the Holy Spirit within us. As we intentionally give him access to our hearts by spending time in his presence and in his word, God himself will begin to change us from the inside out.

Holiness is an awesome calling but it is our calling. When we refuse to live like we belong to God, we are either telling the world that he is not good or that he is not worth our full allegiance. If I have discovered anything it's that he is both.

Discussion questions

1. What comes to your mind when you hear the word holiness? Read Mark 2:15. How does this snapshot of Jesus' life compare to the common perception of holiness?

2. What is holiness? How does it look in daily life? How can we cultivate lives that demonstrate this kind of holiness?

3. If God has already accepted us on the basis of what Jesus did on the cross, why does holiness matter?

4. If we, as God's people, do not live holy lives, what will be the impact on (a) our relationship with God, (b) the people around us and (c) the role we play in his story?

9 Living like you belong to God

If we do not run our belief about God into practical issues,
it is all up with the vision God has given. The only way
to be obedient to the heavenly vision is to give our utmost
for God's highest, and this can only be done by continually and
resolutely recalling the vision. The test is the sixty seconds
of every minute, and the sixty minutes of every hour,
not our times of prayer and devotional meetings.
(Oswald Chambers)[1]

A man had three servants. Before he left on a long journey he entrusted to each servant some of his inheritance. While he was gone two of the servants worked hard with what they had been given, carefully investing it, so that when their master returned they were able to give him twice what had been placed in their care. The third servant took a different approach. He took his share of the money and buried it in the ground. Hidden beneath the dirt it was safe from harm and would not be lost or stolen, but neither would it grow. On the master's return the servant gave back his share and waited to be praised. To his surprise the master was unimpressed.

Because the first two servants had been faithful with a small amount, their responsibility was increased. However, as he turned to the third servant, the master's face showed not approval, but disappointment. Even his small amount was taken away and entrusted instead to the others, who understood that what they were given was to be used and invested. Their task had never been to hide it away, but to use it in the master's service. Jesus told this story in Matthew 25 to illustrate a lesson that so many of us need to learn. Whether it is the gifts and talents unique to individuals or the life of the kingdom that is our common inheritance, all that God entrusts to his people is given for a purpose. When we take what God has given and bury it in our churches or Bible studies, or even in our minds, we miss completely the task to which we have been called.

It was always God's intention that the law, which revealed his character, would be taken and hammered out on the anvil of everyday life. The proof of the Israelites' relationship with God would be the lives they lived in the homes and markets and fields that were their world.

One of the surprises of Deuteronomy is the broad spectrum of daily life it covers. While God was intimately involved in every area, we are going to dip briefly into three that recur repeatedly throughout the book: marriage, business and care for the poor. Three snapshots from the family album. Three cameos that help us see a little better the kind of people God calls us to be today.

Marriage

Marriage has always been central to God's plan for mankind. It began when God took a rib from Adam's side and made from it a companion whose skills would complement his as they worked together in their common, God-given purpose. As Matthew Henry so beautifully put it, 'The woman was made of a rib out of the side of Adam; not made out of his head to rule over him, nor out of his feet to be trampled upon by him, but out of his side to be equal with him, under his arm to be protected, and near his heart to be beloved.'[2] Created by a God who lived in perfect relationship himself, marriage was designed not only as a reflection of the harmony within the Godhead, but also as the best basis for raising children and building families who knew and feared him.

Long before the Israelites reached the plains of Moab, men and women were no longer living as complementary halves of a perfect whole. The image of God became more and more blurred as they continued to misunderstand and devalue each other. In Israel, and to a staggering degree in the surrounding nations, women had little value. Many of the laws God gave to Israel address that imbalance. To the listeners they were revolutionary. While in other societies unfaithfulness was tolerated in men and carried the death penalty for women, for the Israelites holiness in marriage left no room for double standards. Again and again throughout Deuteronomy God is clear about the absolute requirement for sexual purity among his people.

Not only were God's people to demonstrate his faithfulness in their commitment to one another, but they were to go further and treat one another in a way that reflected his character. No longer were men able to set aside their wives lightly, humiliating them and leaving them destitute. Instead they were to be loyal, compassionate and faithful for life. Similarly, women who found themselves with a new freedom were reminded that it was not licence to treat their husbands with anything less than the absolute respect and honour due a partner who, like them, was made in the image of God himself.

The seriousness of the laws themselves are a stark reminder of the importance God places on marriage and the covenant on which it is based. By holding them to the highest standard, the God who understood his people was calling them to a commitment which would provide protection and stability, not only for individuals and families, but ultimately for the nation itself.

We live in a world where the commitment required in marriage often takes second place to our feelings. I have sat many times with people whose lives have been devastated by spouses who have abandoned their families because they no longer 'feel happy'. When life gets tough and children demand attention, when work is endless and laughter doesn't come as easily as it used to, when someone younger begins to take notice and makes you feel the way you used to, the temptation is to run. When we do that, giving in to the lie that our temporary happiness is the highest goal, we sacrifice more than we could ever gain. In contrast, when we put the happiness of others above our own, we can find ourselves surprised by a depth of joy that can be discovered in even the most unlikely places.

Sadly, God's intention for marriage has been the subject of great misunderstanding over the centuries. Truth has been twisted to justify behaviour that is utterly at odds with his character. I witnessed the impact of these misconceptions recently in the life of a lady I will call Sarah. I got to know Sarah when she joined a Bible study group of which I was part. As we went through the book of Ephesians together Sarah was happy to join in and make comments, until we came to Ephesians 5 where Paul begins to talk about marriage. At that point her attitude changed completely. A difficult childhood and a broken marriage of her own had left her hostile to what she considered to be the Biblical view of marriage. Before we even began to read the verses her defences were firmly up.

Over the following couple of weeks we looked together at the reality of God's plan for marriage. Taking the heart of the laws in Deuteronomy, Paul puts them in the light of the life of Jesus. In fact, he points out that the responsibility of husbands to love their wives is the same sacrificial love that was displayed by Jesus himself on the cross.

It was moving to watch Sarah's defences come down as she gradually discovered that God's plan for marriage was very different to what she had experienced in her own life. Rather than an excuse for men to dominate and control their wives, she began to see that the leadership given to them in marriage was actually intended as a powerful demonstration of the same sacrificial love that Jesus displayed on the cross. Whether husband or wife, to love as God intended was to live as Jesus lived, seeking not to be served but to serve.

Within the space of a few weeks Sarah's perspective had changed radically. Instead of her initial hostility, she openly admitted her longing to experience the mutual support, respect, partnership and love that lay at the heart of God's plan for marriage. While it was thrilling to watch the transformation that took place in Sarah's life, I found it deeply saddening to realize that she had never seen an authentic demonstration of biblical marriage.

For those of us who are married, do our marriages paint an accurate picture of the love of God? Do our spouses see God's heart in action as we sacrificially love them, regardless of feelings? Do our children watch the way we interact and see in it his grace? Do our neighbours see something different in the care and respect we show for one another? If not, why not?

If marriage as God intended reflects his love to a watching world, then it should not surprise us that it is the frontline in the war against selfishness. It is, however, a war that we must commit ourselves to fighting. When we allow our marriages to be destroyed by satisfying our own egos, we take the image of God and deface it before a world that needs to see his glory.

Business

The second snapshot we are going to consider is the area of business. For many people the fact that a book like Deuteronomy has anything to say about business comes as a surprise.

We live in a society that has divorced Christian service from the 'secular' world. I remember sitting in church one day as we prayed together for a group of young people who were heading overseas on a mission team. It was so encouraging to hear of all that they and their friends would do over the two-week period and I was looking forward to hearing a report on their return. On the way out I passed a man who runs a substantial business in our area. At a time when the financial climate was difficult and the jobs of a large number of people were in his hands, he faced the task of living out God's standards in the most testing of circumstances. I couldn't help but wonder who, on this occasion, had the harder task. Why is it that we consider going on a mission team or working for a church 'Christian service', while running a business or being a teacher or working in a supermarket are somehow less spiritual? When we view life in this way we do two things.

Firstly, we devalue the significant roles that the majority of Christians play in our world. We forget that only a small minority are called to overseas mission or to full-time church or Christian work. These are crucial roles, but they play only one part in God's plan for his people. The idea that secular and sacred life can be separated was totally unfamiliar to the Israelites and is something we adopted much later from the Greeks. The impact of a person who is prepared to know their God and live his heart in ordinary, everyday life cannot be underestimated.

Secondly, we encourage the notion that the standards expected in the workplace are less or different from those expected elsewhere. As the Israelites began to understand God's law it became clear that their responsibility to reflect the character of God was as central to business life as it was to life in the temple.

Not long ago I heard about a man who, after a twenty-year business relationship, discovered that his colleague was a Christian. Despite being an active member of his local church, not once in twenty years had the man's attitude or behaviour given any indication that he was different. Like the third servant in Jesus' story, he was content to bury his faith, keeping it safe for a Sunday morning. Not only did he totally misunderstand what it meant to live as part of God's kingdom, he left his friend questioning the reality of his relationship with God.

God's law made it clear to the Israelites that their relationship with him must translate into the reality of their working life. As people of their word they were to be careful to follow through on what they said (Deuteronomy 23:21–23). They were to be men and women of integrity, not having different standards depending on who they were dealing with (Deuteronomy 25:13–16). Even in business they were to be people of compassion, allowing their success to benefit others. Whether they were gathering the harvest in the fields, from the olive trees or in their vineyards, any produce missed the first time round was left to be collected by those in need (Deuteronomy 24:19–21).

As members of the nation of Israel, employers would have no right to oppress their servants. Chapter 24 makes it clear that God has no place for those who take advantage of people in need of work. Whether Israelites or foreigners, employees had to be treated fairly. Wages were to be paid at the end of the day in the knowledge that they were relied upon to feed a family.

In a hard-nosed business culture like ours, even the provisions regarding loans are a startling contrast. When a loan was made it was made against a pledge, much like our modern-day guarantees. The law is clear that any pledge taken should not place an unnecessary burden on the borrower or place them under additional financial strain (Deuteronomy 24:6). In fact, even when a pledge had to be collected, it was to be done in a way that demonstrated compassion. Rather than going inside the home, where the man's family would witness his humiliation, the pledge was to be taken quietly outside (Deuteronomy 24:11). In this way the dignity of the debtor would be preserved. Going one step further, if the item in question was a cloak, it was to be returned at nightfall so that the debtor would not have to sleep without it (Deuteronomy 24:13).

What kind of a God is so intimately interested in the lives of his people that protecting someone who is on the bottom rung of society from the chill of a winter night ranks above profit? If that is the character of God, what does he want our motivation in business to be? If the heart of God is to be central to every aspect of life, then the onus is on the men and women of our business world to know their God and conduct their business in a way that is true to his character.

Care for the poor

The third snapshot of life as God's people is the practical concern the Israelites were to show for those in need. Obedience to God's law would be a practical demonstration, not only of God's love, but of their understanding that all they had came from God. They were to live as a nation who treated people in keeping with their God, rather than their status, caring and providing for widows, orphans and even the foreigners among them.

Also, built into the life of the nation of Israel was a time at the end of every seven years when all debt would be cancelled. Instead of an endless cycle of poverty, those who had fallen on difficult times would have an opportunity to start again with a clean slate. Not only was their debt to be released but it was to be done freely and ungrudgingly. Similar provisions applied where, as the result of poverty, an Israelite was forced to sell themselves into slavery. In the seventh year they were to be set free with generous provisions which would enable them to start a new life. In both situations obedience came at a financial cost. God called his people to have generous hearts and added a promise that he would bless them in return.

Deuteronomy 15:4–5 makes an astonishing claim: 'There will be no poor among you, since the LORD will surely bless you in the land which the LORD your God is giving you an inheritance to possess, if only you listen obediently to the voice of the LORD your God, to observe carefully all this commandment which I am commanding you today.' If the Israelites obeyed everything God told them to do they would end up with a society entirely without poverty. Can you imagine if a politician today made a claim like that? Yet, made by a God who had proved himself utterly trustworthy, it was a statement that could be taken seriously. While poverty and struggle is a reality in our world it has never been God's plan for mankind. His people cannot turn a blind eye to it.

While it grieves the heart of God, the silent scream of a world in need is all too often unheard or even ignored by his people. We do not have to travel to the Third World to find poverty. Within our own neighbourhoods and communities are people who are struggling, not only with poverty, but with addiction, abuse, grief, depression, loneliness and more. If we are going to live lives that reflect the heart of God then the things that move him must in turn move us. Whether it is by sacrificing our time, opening our home, sharing our food, giving our money or simply offering friendship, the more we understand the character of God, the more it will move us to action.

While some of the provisions in Deuteronomy may require some deciphering, the requirement to care practically for those in need is not limited by culture. It is not difficult to understand what it means to care for widows, orphans and the poor. The problem is that understanding it is not enough. Speaking to the church in the New Testament, James said, 'Suppose a brother or sister is without clothes and daily food, if one of you says to him, "Go, I wish you well; keep warm and well fed" but does nothing about his physical needs, what good is it? In the same way, faith by itself, if it is not accompanied by action, is dead' (James 2:15–17). Whether it was in marriage, business, community, family, justice, conservation or any of the other aspects of ordinary life the law of God covers, their understanding of it had to translate into practical reality.

For me, the difficulty is not writing these words. The test comes when the quiet hum of my computer is replaced by the slamming of the front door and the voices of my children. When my husband's needs are different from my own and my well-fed ego fights against God's call to put my husband first. It comes when money is tight and it is easy to justify my decision not to share it. Similarly, the challenge to you is not to simply read God's word but to let it transform the way you live. Whatever area of life we find ourselves in, if our understanding of God's call does not cause us to cultivate a godly life, then all we have is empty knowledge.

It was never God's plan for his people to live like the third servant in Jesus' story. If they listened to or even read the law and then chose to hide it away, dealing with the practical reality of life in their own way, they would miss the point entirely. However, if they understood that they were not only to know God's law, but to apply it in every situation they faced, their everyday lives would be transformed and God's character would be revealed to a watching world.

Discussion questions

1. Read Romans 12:1–2. What does Paul urge the believers to do? How would it affect their lives? If we were to live like this, how would it impact us?

2. In what ways was marriage designed to reflect the character of God? When marriage breaks down, how does it affect (a) individuals, (b) society and (c) people's perception of God?

3. To what extent can the business practices of the twenty-first-century Christian reflect the heart of God? What difficulties are likely to arise?

4. Read Matthew 25:34–40. How does God expect his people to treat those in need? What are some of the ways we can practically obey this command of God?

10 Choosing life

Choice: (noun) an act of choosing between
two or more possibilities.
(Oxford Dictionaries)[1]

Finally, the moment had arrived. The time for theory was over. The time for action had come. The character of God and the words he had spoken demanded a response and it was time for the Israelites to make their choice. The last few verses of Deuteronomy 26 record the beautiful declarations made by God and his people as they confirm again the covenant that binds them together. The declaration made by the nation of Israel as they respond to the call of their God is summed up by Moses, 'You have declared this day that the LORD is your God and that you will walk in his ways, that you will keep his decrees, commands and laws, and that you will obey him' (Deuteronomy 26:17).

In that moment, as the seeds of centuries of hope take root within their hearts, the people of Israel commit to follow and obey their God. The promises he makes to them are staggering. They will be his people, a treasured possession made for fame, honour and praise. They will be set apart for holiness, just as he has promised.

In any other story this would be the moment the credits begin to roll. As we finished our popcorn and reached for our coats we would feel a sense of satisfaction. The familiar tale has been well told. A hero is plucked from obscurity and, after some tense battles against the enemy and a resounding victory, he and his people stride into a free world. But this isn't any other story. This is life.

When the Israelites declared that they would follow God it was only the beginning. The choice they made was not just for that moment, as joy buoyed their spirits and hope made them brave. It was not a one-off decision, but the first step on a lifelong commitment to obedience. It was a vow whose authenticity would be proved in the minutes and hours of everyday life.

This first decision, while important, was not the most difficult one. The choices that followed would really test their allegiance to their God. Because he knew how quickly they would forget, God gave the Israelites a physical reminder of the choice that was continually before them.

In the Promised Land, towering on the skyline, were two mountains, Mount Ebal and Mount Gerizim. As the nation of Israel entered the land that God had promised them they were to divide into two groups. One group would stand on Mount Ebal and the other on Mount Gerizim. One represented the curses which came with disobedience to the law of God. The other represented obedience. As the Levites read out the list of curses, the suffering that God longed to spare his people, they would verbally confirm that they understood and accepted the consequences of disobedience. Then they would listen with awe as God reminded them of the blessings he would shower upon them if they chose to live as he commanded.

Can you imagine the emotion of that day? Can you picture what it was like to stand on one of those mountains, your feet on ground you had only ever dreamt about, listening as the Levites read the list of curses and blessings, adding your voice to the millions who understood the importance of obedience? Such a day would not be easily forgotten. As the years passed, just the sight of those peaks in the distance would evoke a flood of memories. Even for future generations the mountains would bring to mind the stories of that day.

The choice that faced the Israelites on the plains of Moab, and every day which followed, was so important that God embedded it into the fabric of their inheritance. As they looked at Mount Gerizim they would be reminded of the blessings of God that would be theirs when they were obedient to his law, walking with him and understanding his heart. Mount Ebal, on the other hand, would remind them of a second possibility. By rejecting God's law and going their own way the people could make a very different choice. They could choose life without God, which in reality is death. When their heartfelt vow began to seem less important, the mountains themselves cried out in warning, their constant presence a tangible reminder of the importance of obedience.

When my daughter Lara was very small the day came when she decided she could get dressed by herself. She had let me help her for long enough and now she could do it on her own. For the most part it worked out well. We had the odd back-to-front t-shirt or mismatched sock but generally it was a success. The exception was her cardigans. What had once been just another part of her wardrobe became her nemesis. Each time she would think she had finally got it right, but when she got to the last button there would be no hole. Or there would be a hole but no button. A red-head, with the stubbornness to match, she refused to allow me to help. There were stamping feet and shouts of frustration until eventually she sat down on the floor and began to cry. That was when we came up with a plan. Before Lara tried to do up her cardigan she would come to me and I would fasten the top button. She discovered that when the top button was in place the rest began to make sense.

God knew that unless his people put him first life would get out of control. Instead of the life they were created for, they would find themselves in a mess. Instead of fulfilment they would end up with frustration and pain. Instead of serving the Lord 'joyfully and gladly' (Deuteronomy 28:47), they would end up serving their enemies 'in hunger and thirst, in nakedness and dire poverty' (Deuteronomy 28:48). Instead of defeating their enemies and possessing the land of their inheritance, they would end up scattered from one end of the earth to the other, serving gods of wood and stone who could neither feel their pain nor answer their cries for help.

God is not secretive about the importance of this choice. He does not try to trick his people into commitment. The choice is clear and so are the consequences. When the time came and the people of Israel found themselves in the very situations they had been warned about, when their barns were empty and enemies were closing in, they found themselves without excuse.

As he calls them to choose, God reminds his people that the choice set before them is not too difficult. It is not out of their reach. Nor is it a choice someone can make on their behalf. It is not found in some mysterious quest but in the words of the God who calls them to live.

If there is one passage that sums up the heart of Deuteronomy and in many ways God's desire for his people from that time until now, it is found in chapter 30 verses 19 and 20:

I call heaven and earth to witness against you today, that I
have set before you life and death, the blessing and the curse.
So *choose life* in order that you may live, you and your
descendants, by loving the LORD your God, by obeying his
voice, and by holding fast to him.
(NASB, my emphasis)

Can you imagine the urgency of these words, from the heart
of a God who longed for his people to experience life? Spoken
by a man who had dedicated his own to leading them home?
This was not a monotone address from a dusty pulpit but an
impassioned plea that carried the weight of a message of
unparalleled importance.

To choose life was not an intellectual decision. It was a
practical commitment, lived out in three ways:

1. Loving the Lord your God
2. Obeying his voice
3. Holding fast to him.

In a world that uses love to describe the fickle nature of
celebrity relationships, the physical attraction that comes and
goes in a night and even our feelings towards soap or tooth-
paste, it is difficult to understand what it means to love the
Lord your God.

Love is not a wave of emotion or a warm feeling. It is not
something that comes upon you and then leaves again at an
unexpected moment. It is not passive and it is not transient.
It may help to understand that, in Hebrew thought, to hate
can mean to put in second place, or to love less. In contrast,
to love is to put first.

To love God is an intentional decision. If we simply wait
for emotion to swell within our hearts we may wait for a long

time. If we allow ourselves to behave simply on the basis of our feelings we will be blown around like leaves on the breeze. Only when we intentionally commit to knowing him, allowing his heart to transform the way we live, will we be overwhelmed by the sheer beauty of who he is. Our feelings towards God are not the motivation to spend time in his presence: they are the result of doing so. If you want to love God, open his word and get to know him. Whether you feel like it or not. As you grow to know him you will find yourself in the grip of a love that will change your life and set your heart on fire.

The second way to choose life is through obedience. In a society where the law was read aloud, repetition was an indication that the subject matter was extremely important. Just as a parent will repeat an important instruction until their child has understood it, there are areas of the law that come up again and again. If we keep coming back to the subject of obedience it is because it was, and still is, the basis of an intimate relationship with God. In John 14:21 Jesus says, 'Whoever has my commands and obeys them, he is the one who loves me.' For us, as for the Israelites, love and obedience cannot be separated. What does obedience look like in your everyday life? How does it affect the decisions you make as you get up in the morning, get home from work or relax with your friends? To choose life is intentionally to live in obedience to God's word, whatever situation you find yourself in. John goes on to put it even more strongly: 'The man who says, "I know him," but does not do what he commands is a liar.' (1 John 2:4). If we truly want to live as the people of God, to understand and play our part in his story, obedience to his word is not optional.

The third part of choosing life is holding fast; the courageous and unwavering commitment to stand as his no matter what comes your way. Whether prosperity and blessing tempt you to go it alone, or the struggle to get by has left you weary and disillusioned, don't let go. Whether your days are filled with laughter, or pain and loss threaten to engulf you: I implore you, hold fast. Whatever life brings, when we commit to hold on to God and who he is, we will discover that we are not holding on in our own strength. When we take hold of him we find our hand engulfed in his, and his is a grip that will hold through any storm.

May Morrow knew what it was to hold fast. She had suffered in her later years from motor neurone disease, a cruel condition that robs the sufferer of every bodily function leaving them a prisoner in their own body until eventually it takes their life. At her funeral I heard how May, a woman who loved to talk and chat, had eventually lost even her speech. No longer able to communicate and barely able to hold a pencil in her shaking hand, she slowly formed on a page the words 'I'm still trusting'. How was May able to hold fast even in those circumstances? She held fast because she was able to trust a God she knew. That kind of trust does not come from intellectual knowledge but from a relationship that is born out of obedience. It comes from a lifetime of following God and listening to his voice.

The richness of life in relationship with God would not follow automatically from a decision made in a solemn, emotionally charged moment on the plains of Moab. In order to live as he intended, the Israelites had to continually choose life.

As Deuteronomy draws to a close it marks the end of the life of Moses, an extraordinary man who taught the people the law of God and is described as knowing the Lord face to face like no-one who has lived since.

Before he died Moses taught the people of Israel a song that reminded them of their story. It was a declaration of the character of their God. As they sang it they would remember again all that God had been to them, and all he in turn called them to be. They would be reminded again of his faithfulness, and of the consequences they would face if they turned their back on him. As Moses passed the mantle of leadership to Joshua, who would lead them into the land, the people were equipped with all they needed to possess their inheritance and live the life to which they were called.

If they obeyed the law, the Israelites would not only be protected from the dangers they faced, they would live lives marked out by holiness. As they understood the law, they would begin to know the God whose character it reflected and whose presence was among them. The fear of God which grew with their knowledge of him would inspire them to choose obedience, and that obedience would lead them into all that God intended for them.

Moses left behind a people who belonged to God. Before they set a foot in the Promised Land he called them his. The choice they faced was not whether to become the people of God; they already were. The choice was whether they would live accordingly. For now they had chosen life. The reality of that commitment would be tested in the years that lay ahead.

For us, the real test of our commitment to follow God is not in the services we attend or the emotion we feel. Our faith will be proved in the moments and days when we are assaulted by the temptation to settle for less. When bitterness is an easier alternative to forgiveness. When love is more difficult than hate. When Bible study is less appealing than television or the internet. When the pull of a warm bed wrestles with the desire to begin the day in God's presence. These are the moments when we choose life.

Discussion questions

1. Read Deuteronomy 30:11–20. As Moses spoke to the nation of Israel, already secure in their position as the people of God, what did it mean for them to choose life? How does this apply to Christians today?

2. What does it mean to love God? What will be the result of a devotion based purely on feelings? If love is an intentional choice, how can we practically choose to love God?

3. Read 1 John 2:3–6. How is obedience linked to love? What is indicated by lack of obedience?

4. In Hebrews 10:23 the writer picks up the theme of holding fast, encouraging the believers to 'hold unswervingly to the hope we profess, for he who promised is faithful'. Where do we find the strength to hold fast? What does it mean to hold fast in everyday life?

11 The heart of the problem

I know their intent which they are developing today,
before I have brought them into the land.
(Deuteronomy 31:21 NASB)

The end of Deuteronomy marks a turning point for the people of Israel. Centuries of waiting were finally over. As the nation dismantled their vast camp and crossed the Jordan River into Canaan they discovered – again – that God was as good as his word. Joshua's astonishing victories left their enemies trembling in the presence of the God of Israel and reminded his people that his covenants are unbreakable.

Armed with the promises of God, led by his presence and grounded in his law, the Israelites were finally able to possess the inheritance God had given them. Under the leadership of Joshua the people of God finally made it home.

The story of life in the Promised Land makes for fascinating reading. This is no sanitized, tidy, feel-good tale. As well as the history itself, we are given glimpses of the struggles and searching questions of people whose lives are as real as the God who calls them. To try to cover in one chapter the story that fills the remainder of the Old Testament would be like trying to fit the Pacific Ocean into a thimble. However, before we go on to consider the impact of Jesus on the unfolding story, it is vital that we stop for just a moment to consider what became of the nation of Israel. Did the law that held so much promise bring them the life they dreamt of?

As they began to put down roots in Canaan it is hard to imagine that their loyalty to God would even come into question. With their experience of him, all that they had learned along the way, how could their hearts not be anchored in God? Surely rebellion would be only a distant memory?

While Joshua and the others who knew and obeyed God's word remained alive, the nation did for a time experience the blessings of their inheritance. After Joshua died the nation of Israel began to release their hold on the one who would have held them fast. Despite God's presence in the tabernacle, despite the song and the law and the warnings, things quickly began to go wrong. As the law was pushed to the side new generations grew up who knew nothing of God.

Recently, during a heavy snowfall, I had to drive my daughters to school. As I attempted to manoeuvre round a small roundabout the wheels slipped and we slid sideways into the kerb. The bump was only small and we were soon on our way again, believing no damage had been done. It wasn't until a couple of days later that I noticed something odd. As I drove down the long straight road that leads into our town the car kept pulling in to the side. Unknown to me something had been damaged. Unless it was continually corrected the car kept veering off the road.

It was like that with the Israelites. As their history progressed there were times when they walked with God and obeyed his law. There were many more when they took a different path entirely. Times when they allowed themselves to be led by the surrounding nations or simply by their own rebellious hearts until they had all but forgotten their God, his laws and the purpose for which he had called them.

If the Israelites, as God's chosen people, were not able to enter fully into the life they were offered, what was the reason? Did obedience to the law not produce the life God had promised? When you look at the relationship between the life of Israel and their obedience to the law, one thing becomes clear. The problem was not God's faithfulness, nor was it the effectiveness of the law he gave them. Just as he had promised, every time his people returned wholeheartedly to obedience, God blessed them.

The problem that repeatedly kept them from obeying his voice was one God had understood from the beginning. Despite their best intentions, the selfishness and rebellion that was so deeply rooted in their hearts would eventually lead them away from him. Even as they made their declarations on the plains of Moab, God knew that the people he loved would betray him. He knew their hearts would draw them away. In the same way that my car kept pulling off the road, the natural inclination of mankind has always been to go our own way.

One of the things that changed my life and my understanding of God forever was the realization that the Old Testament is a masterpiece that points from the very first word to the coming of Jesus. Every brush-stroke in the story of God's people paints a picture of the one who would bring together all they had been taught and all they had been preparing for.

If you believe that Jesus appears first in the pages of Matthew, you need to look again at the Old Testament. A lifetime of study would not begin to unpack all the references that point to him and yet each new discovery will give a deeper appreciation of who he is. To try to understand the big story only in the light of the New Testament is as impossible as understanding a great novel by reading only the final chapter.

Even as you move from Joshua into Judges, the cycle of rebellion and remorse that would continue to blight the nation makes it clear that something more is needed. As God's law is sidelined, his people are drawn to the things they have been warned against. Again and again they veer off track and find themselves unable to enjoy the land of their inheritance or the God who gave it to them. Each time, with unparalleled patience, God raised up people who were prepared to obey. People like the judges, who were used to draw Israel back to him. Even in these dark days, as the nation rebelled and famine ravaged the Promised Land, there was always a light in the darkness. In a breathtaking picture of what was to come, the beautiful story of Ruth reminded the Israelites that people whose decisions left them destitute could be redeemed, set free, by a brother who was prepared to pay the price to give them back their life. One day God would come, not just as the final judge, raised up to save the nation, but as the brother who was prepared to pay the ultimate price to give them life.

In an attempt to be like the nations around, Israel eventually rejected God as their king. Despite God's warnings, they wanted a man who would reign over them. Instead of being set apart as a holy nation, governed by the Most High God, they chose to be just like everyone else. Instead of walking with God they chose to take direction from a man whose nature was as flawed as their own. Amazingly, before they rebelled and clamoured for a human king to lead them, God had set in place laws to protect them in this choice. Even in their unfaithfulness God remained faithful. If the man appointed to rule over Israel would set his heart on God he could actually lead the people back into obedience. In effect, he could remind the people that God was their true king.

Saul, the first king of Israel, was far from that ideal. In contrast David, the second king, was a man after God's own heart. As you read the psalms that David wrote, his delight in God's law is infectious. He was a man who understood the source of deep joy and yet he also experienced real pain and real failure. He was the king against whom all future kings would be measured. Yet David still fell far short of all that God desired him to be. Despite his love of God's law and his desire for holiness, David made spectacular mistakes. Even the greatest king of Israel was not the answer to the problem. Only when God himself came, born as a baby in the line of David, would a king have the power to bring the people back to God.

We have already come across King Solomon, David's son. Solomon began well. During his reign he built the temple that became the dwelling of God among his people, just as the tabernacle had been in the wilderness years. Solomon's wisdom was legendary and people came from far and wide to listen to him. Sadly, to begin well is not enough. Despite his immense wisdom, riches beyond imagining and the example of his father before him, Solomon did not hold fast to God. After marrying women of other nations he quickly began to worship their gods. When their leader was not committed to following God, the nation followed suit.

Things went from bad to worse for God's people after Solomon died. Their rejection of God led to the nation being divided. The ten tribes in the north of the land became Israel and were drawn into the worship of idols by the insecurity and arrogance of King Jeroboam. A succession of kings, each one more defiant than the last, drew Israel deeper into the life of idolatry that they had been warned against and the consequences were just as God had said. The two tribes to the south, now known as Judah, were led by Solomon's son Rehoboam. A nation created to display the glory of God became divided against itself.

Even then, God did not abandon Israel. Through the prophets he continually warned his people and gave them opportunities to return to him and to the life which had captivated them on the plains of Moab. Before he removed them from the land that had held so much promise, God reminded them again of all that could be theirs if they returned to obedience.

To Israel he sent Hosea, a man whose marriage was a vivid and painful picture of the way God's people had broken their covenant. The people watched as Hosea struggled repeatedly with his wife's unfaithfulness, and as his children suffered the consequences of their mother's abandonment. Through Hosea's life God showed them the awful reality of their unfaithfulness and the consequences that would follow.

When God shocked his people by sending Jonah to the barbaric city of Nineveh, he challenged their spiritual smugness with a reminder that his love was not just for them. The purpose of God's people had always been to turn the nations to him. Again, through Amos and Nahum and Obadiah a patient God laid his heart before the nation he loved.

To Judah he sent Joel, Isaiah, Micah, Zephaniah, Jeremiah and Habakkuk. Message after message of warning and reminder, all falling on deaf ears. A nation who set out with a declaration that they would be the people of God became so steeped in the world around them that they could no longer hear his voice.

We have already discovered that the holiness and love of God will not let disobedience, or the pain it causes, continue forever. It was no different for the nation of Israel. Finally, the time came when the holiness of God demanded that they were removed from the land which had offered so much hope. The inheritance that was theirs was squandered through disobedience. In his sovereignty, God allowed Israel to be captured by Assyria and carried into captivity, followed later by Judah, captured by the Babylonians. The people of God were scattered. The temple that enabled their holy God to live among them was destroyed. A nation who were spectacularly rescued from Egypt by the God who gave them hope chose, through a progression of seemingly small decisions, to return to slavery.

Through it all, even in captivity, there were still glimpses of hope. People such as Daniel who stood as men of God, refusing to follow the crowd. When all seemed lost God always had a place for those who were prepared to listen to his heart and walk in his ways. Despite everything, the God who had known his people would betray him refused to give up on them. The God who cannot break his covenant continued to pursue relentlessly the heart of the nation he loved.

After a period in exile a remnant of the Israelites was able to return to Jerusalem. 1 and 2 Chronicles tells the story of the nation as they looked at their history and rebellion with the benefit of hindsight, and wondered if there was hope. Could they really once again be the people of God? As is always the case, when people genuinely ask that question before God, the answer was a resounding yes.

Under the direction of Ezra and Nehemiah, the temple and walls of Jerusalem were rebuilt and the people returned once again to obedience. God also remained faithful to his people scattered among the other nations. At the same time as the walls of Jerusalem were being rebuilt God prepared Esther, a Jewish girl, to marry King Xerxes, the ruler of a territory stretching from India to Ethiopia. In becoming queen she was able to stop a plot that would have destroyed the Jewish people.

Whether they returned to the Promised Land or lived out their calling among the other nations, the Israelites were never abandoned by their God. Haggai, Zechariah and Malachi give us more insight into the relationship between God and his people during the years following their return from exile. However badly it affected their intimacy and walk with God, no rebellion or rejection could ever cause him to break his covenant.

Not only did God remain faithful to his word, but through it all he continued to whisper the promise that something more was coming. Even as they stood on the plains of Moab, full of declarations they could not keep, God promised that one day he would deal with their hearts. Even during their years of exile God spoke these words through the prophet Ezekiel:

> I will give you a new heart and put a new spirit in you; I will remove from you your heart of stone and give you a heart of flesh. And I will put my Spirit in you and move you to follow my decrees and be careful to keep my laws.
> (Ezekiel 36:26–27)

The day was coming when God himself would show them how to live the law they could not keep. Instead of being inscribed on stone tablets it would be written on their hearts. The God who had to continually draw them back would fix the problem that caused them to stray. In a way that even the judges, the kings and the prophets could never do, he himself would give them the power to obey.

Sometimes I find it hard to read the story of the nation of Israel without getting frustrated. How could they miss it? How could a nation who had heard the voice of God reflect his character so poorly? How could people who had been given the law that could transform their society just cast it aside? How could they have been given so much and yet love him so little?

It's so easy to condemn them for their disobedience. To shake my head at the absence of holiness and rail against their lack of love. It's easy to fool myself into believing I would have stood with Joshua, or later with those who went against the crowd and clung to their God. But would I? Really?

If we stop and look around our world, or even our churches, what do we see? There will always be those who stand for God. Dotted in the unlikely places there will be hearts that understand their king and serve him with a passion that will not be swayed. They are not in the majority. Despite the riches of what we have in Christ, as a church we are failing dismally to reflect the holiness of our God. In us his image is all too often tattered and veiled.

We owe a debt of gratitude to the Jewish people we can never repay. The life of the nation of Israel has been used by God to help us understand not only who he is, but what he wants his people to be. Without Israel we would not have the pictures of Christ that show him to be beautiful beyond our most eloquent words. We would understand neither why we are totally unable to be holy without him nor why he satisfies the deepest needs of our heart. If we fail to understand and be drawn into the story of the kingdom, we will miss the stunning significance of the moment when God became man.

Discussion questions

1. Read Isaiah 29:13. What was the problem for the nation of Israel? How was their relationship with God's law affected?

2. Just as God had repeatedly warned, what were the consequences of disobedience for the nation as a whole?
3. According to Ezekiel 36:26–27, how was God going to deal with the rebellion in their hearts? How would this impact their relationship with God's law?
4. Read 2 Chronicles 16:9 and Isaiah 51:7–8. What is God's response to individuals who choose to put him first, regardless of what is happening around them?

12 The Word became flesh

. . . the God who speaks in the Old Testament,
who entered into covenant with his people Israel,
and inspired and moved the prophets, was none
other than the God known in Jesus Christ.
God has not changed or evolved.
Jesus Christ was always at the heart of God.
(Bruce Milne)[1]

Despite his apparent silence, during their 400 years of slavery in Egypt the Israelites still had a promise that their God would not abandon them. A promise that the God who had proved himself faithful in the past would remain faithful in the present. Similarly, 400 years after God last spoke through the prophet Malachi, his people were still scanning the horizon for their rescuer. Waiting for the 'something more' that God had promised. Listening for the prophet who would speak the words which made them tremble at Sinai, yet in a way their human minds could comprehend.

When that rescue came it was something not even the Jews, in their intimate relationship with God, dared believe possible.

Even the nation who had known his presence in the temple, and had seen his heart in the beauty of his law, were not prepared for the way he came into their world.

Familiarity has robbed many of us of the awe that comes with a proper understanding of what the birth of Jesus meant. Year after year we sit in crowded school halls and watch as children with tea towels perched precariously on their heads re-enact the Christmas story. Accompanied by the flicker of candles and the smell of pine, the familiar Scriptures wash over us while Bing Crosby croons idly in the recesses of our consciousness. The truth is, when we put the story of Jesus' birth in a box with decorations and leftover wrapping paper, we rob ourselves of a reality which rocked the nation of Israel and changed the course of human history forever.

Rebecca Manley Pippert tells the story of the moment the possibility of the incarnation hit her. As she lay in her back garden on a summer's day, at the age of eighteen, she became aware of two ants which had crawled on to her hand. As she watched them, she began to wonder if they even knew she was there. As the thought developed, she realized how difficult it would be to communicate with them. If she spoke, their fear in her presence would send them scuttling to safety. If she found a way to reassure them, her words would not be understood. It occurred to her that the only way she could ever communicate with the ants would be if she were able to become an ant herself. In that moment she remembered the claim that God had become a man. She was so struck by the implications that she became determined to find out more about the story behind the Christian faith. The journey she embarked on transformed her life.

The gospel of John begins with three words, 'In the beginning'. By using the very words which begin the Hebrew Bible, John places the birth of Jesus in the context of the big story. Those simple words would transport the Jewish mind back to the God of creation and of Sinai, to the God of Abraham, Isaac and Jacob, who had led them out of Egypt and revealed his holiness in the law. Before he introduces Jesus, John reminds his readers that 'the Word' had been at the heart of the story from the very first moment.

Sometimes we subconsciously carry the idea that Jesus was a lesser version of God. That he was a son in the sense of being a junior version of God, coming after his father the way my daughter came after me. The Trinity is a mystery that the human mind will never fully understand, but John does not let us entertain for a moment the notion that the Word was less than God. He was not created or produced by God, but integral to God. He was complete with every aspect of the holy character which had been revealed to Israel. Just as words are used to reveal what is within us, the Word was God revealed. From the beginning and before, the Word was central to the character of God. Central in creation, in the giving of the law and in the leading of his people, he was not only with God, he *was* God.

To understand this truth is to realize that the words of John 1:14 are the most breathtakingly profound ever penned: 'The Word became flesh and made his dwelling among us.' Imagine for a moment that your heart has not been dulled by the familiarity of the story. Put yourself in the shoes of a Jew who had grown up in awe of the God of Sinai. When the trembling Israelites asked a holy God to speak in a way they could understand, do you think they dared imagine he would become one of them? How could they ever dream that the heart of God in all its holiness could beat within the chest of a man? Yet, in Jesus, that is exactly what happened.

Hebrews 1:1–3 tells us that God, who had spoken in so many ways in the past, was now speaking through Jesus. In

Hebrew thought, to be a 'son of' can also mean to have all the characteristics of someone else. Even in that respect, Jesus was the perfect son of God. In his humanity he was 'the radiance of God's glory and the exact representation of his being'. God had lived among his people in the tabernacle, giving them detailed laws to protect them from his unapproachable holiness. Now he would live, or as it can also be translated, 'tabernacle', among them in a very different way. As Jesus, God was not just among them, he was one of them.

The truth of the incarnation went even further. When God took on flesh he did not come as a fully grown man, appearing out of the clouds and demanding the attention of his people. Instead, the creator of the heavens and the earth was pushed into the chill of a Bethlehem night as the breath that created life itself was forced in and out of human lungs. The God whose power overwhelmed the might of Egypt became the very essence of helplessness as his human body took shape inside the womb of a young Jewish girl. The one who carried his people through centuries of history, loving and protecting them every step of the way, lay in his mother's arms, defenceless against the world that he had made.

God entered fully into human life. As he walked on the earth he created, he needed his mother's hand to steady him. The God who formed the complexity of muscle, bone and flesh fell and scraped his knee. Like children through the centuries he learned to recognize colours and to count, to comb his hair and even control his bladder. He played games with his siblings and laughed when he was tickled.

To talk about God in these terms seems incomprehensible and almost irreverent, yet if we are ever to appreciate the wonder of his full humanity we must stop and consider what it really meant. As the staggering truth of what he did begins to dawn on your heart, you can't help but ask why he went to such lengths. The answer is love. He did it because the rebellion of his people meant they could never come into his presence and enjoy the relationship they were created for. He did it because without him the people he loved were lost and totally without hope. He did it because he is, and always has been, love itself. When he chose the name Jesus, meaning 'God saves', he made his intentions clear. In order to save mankind, to restore us to the relationship that is our source of life, the God who called his people to fear him became what they were. By becoming a man he showed us what it meant to be fully human. By becoming what we are he showed us all that we could be.

Even Jesus' birth itself points to a greater purpose for his coming. The God who could have been born anywhere on earth chose to place himself in the humblest of circumstances. His first visitors were shepherds who were more accustomed to celebrating the safe arrival of a baby lamb. Yet, according to John 1:29, that is exactly what they were doing on that night. In a statement as profound as it was shocking, John the Baptist described Jesus as 'the Lamb of God, who takes away the sin of the world!' After centuries of celebrating Passover and observing the sacrificial system God had written into their law, the role of the lamb was clear. The Jewish people had no difficulty understanding that a lamb could take their place. The problem was accepting that God himself would become that lamb.

Sadly, because Jesus came in the way they least expected, many of the Jews missed it. As John 1:11 puts it, 'he came to that which was his own, but his own did not receive him.' Those who had been called to reflect his heart did not recognize it when they saw it. People who were never meant for darkness refused to see the light which pointed to their God. A nation that was looking for a conquering warrior to secure their freedom overlooked the man who would do more than all the soldiers who have ever lived.

When God came to live among his people it was not a bolt from the blue, but the culmination of centuries of preparation. Jesus' Jewish context was not an accident. Only in the light of God's relationship with Israel can we begin to grasp why he had to come. Only against the backdrop of their story can his life and words be properly understood. All that Israel had learned and all that they had seen of God had prepared them for this moment.

The law that was given to Israel on Sinai and reiterated on the plains of Moab was the pattern that shaped the life of Jesus from the very beginning. After eight days, the God who introduced circumcision as the sign of his covenant with Abraham was taken to be circumcised. Luke 2:52 tells us that as time passed, Jesus grew in wisdom and stature and in favour with God and men. The God who spoke the law on Sinai not only learned it as a boy, but obeyed it as a man. In perfect obedience the one who wrote the law now embodied it in all its beauty.

If mankind was ever going to be able to relate to a holy God then only he could show us how. By becoming a man Jesus was able to show the world what it means to live in relationship with his Father. Rather than setting aside the law he had given to his people, he embodied it. The God who gave the law on Sinai became the teacher who, through his human life, revealed its heart.

Discussion questions

1. In Exodus 20, as God began to give the law to Israel and Mount Sinai shook and blazed with fire, the people did not want to come near or listen for fear that they would die. How did the coming of Jesus address this problem?

2. In what ways had the history of the Israelites prepared them for the coming of Jesus?

3. Read John 1:10–11. How did the nation of Israel as a whole respond to the birth of Jesus? Why? In what ways can we be guilty of making the same mistake?

4. Read John 1:1–4, 14 and Hebrews 1:2 again. How do these verses help us understand who Jesus really was?

13 Jesus and the law

To fulfil the Torah
is to breathe the breath of life
into the written word.
(Dwight Pryor)[1]

The story is told of a composer who wrote a beautiful symphony and sent it to a group of musicians to be recorded. Despite their best efforts to interpret the written score they could not capture the full beauty of the music and eventually contacted him in frustration. In answer to their request the composer made the journey to where they lived and played it for them on the same piano they used in their rehearsals. Only when they heard the music played by the hands of the one who wrote it were the musicians able to appreciate its magnificence and recreate it themselves.

On Sinai God gave his people the law, telling them how to live in a way that reflected his character. As Jesus he did so much more. By taking the written word and putting flesh on it he allowed the world to see what the heart of God was really like. As he played his composition with his own hands he revealed the beauty that had been hidden by hearts which simply could not grasp it.

Somehow we have become comfortable with the notion that Jesus was opposed to, or at least disregarded, the law revealed in the Old Testament. Not only is this idea unbiblical, it is completely illogical. When God gave the law it was an outpouring of his love, a picture of his character for a nation called to reflect his holiness. How could God himself break the very law which demonstrated his heart? In doing so he would cease to be God.

In an earlier chapter we picked up on Jesus' statement in Matthew 5:17, when he said he came to fulfil the law, not to abolish it. Rather than bringing the law to an end, Jesus' life was a demonstration of the absolute holiness to which it had always pointed. In perfect obedience he met every requirement of the law. Not only did he obey it down to the smallest detail, he did it with the joy and extravagance that had always been at its heart. Just as every note the composer played joined to show the symphony in all its brilliance, Jesus lived the holiness of God with every breath.

Dwight Pryor,[2] founder of the Centre for Judaic-Christian Studies, suggests another dimension to Jesus' fulfilment of the law. He explains that the words meaning to abolish and fulfil were commonly used in the everyday rabbinic debate that formed an important part of study. If one rabbi believed another had misunderstood the law he would accuse him of *abolishing* it, implying that by undermining it with wrong interpretation, that rabbi was causing followers to break or *abolish* the law. Arguing that he had understood the law correctly, the first rabbi may well reply that he was actually *fulfilling* it. In other words, by correctly interpreting it he was leading people to obey the law as it was intended. Even in this sense, Jesus perfectly fulfilled the law by demonstrating how it should be properly understood. In simple terms he showed the world what a life of obedience to the law should look like.

Of the Jews Jesus interacted with on a daily basis, the best known are probably the Pharisees. They were a highly influential group who had formed in an attempt to retain observance to the law, at a time when the Jewish people were being drawn into the Greek-influenced culture of their day. They were separatists who were utterly devoted to keeping the 613 laws found in the Old Testament. Determined to preserve obedience to the law, they even added more restrictions to protect them from violating the original laws. One group was so committed to avoiding adultery that they refused to look at women at all, becoming renowned for the cuts and bruises that were the physical result of a life lived looking at the ground!

It is interesting to note how much time Jesus spends in debate with the Pharisees. We often have the idea that his frustration with them stemmed from their insistence on keeping the law. However, if it is true that he lived his entire life without breaking a single commandment, then how could he condemn them for trying to do the same? The truth is, he didn't. The problem for the Pharisees was not their determination to obey the law but their understanding of its heart.

It is not surprising that the God who taught his people on Sinai came to earth as a teacher. What he had previously taught the Israelites, he now explained further and demonstrated by example. Often as he spoke Jesus referred to 'the kingdom of God', a concept with which the Jews were familiar. People who were part of a nation which had historically rejected God as their king were invited to live as part of a new kingdom. This kingdom was not geographical in nature, but was made up instead of those who wholeheartedly embraced the rule of God in their lives. As he taught, Jesus took the words he spoke on Sinai and expanded them to reveal the heartbeat of this kingdom.

The best-known words of Jesus were not delivered on Sinai, but on another mountainside. In what has become known as 'The Sermon on the Mount' he began to explain his kingdom. Like the rest of Jesus' life and teaching, the Sermon on the Mount demonstrated that life in the kingdom of God did not go against the law, but beyond it.

Take for example the commandment 'Do not murder'. In God's kingdom this law is more than a prohibition against ending life, it is also a warning to guard the attitude of your heart towards others. Even anger that is allowed to fester can eventually build to become murder and must be addressed at the earliest opportunity. Jesus deals not just with the murder that is the end result but with the anger that is the root of the problem. Adultery is approached in a similar way. Jesus reminds people that the unfaithfulness forbidden by the law begins in a mind which allows wrong desire to build to its inevitable conclusion.

In Matthew 5:38 Jesus takes another law the Jews were familiar with and puts a new slant on it. The term 'an eye for an eye' has entered our everyday vocabulary as licence for revenge. In its context in Deuteronomy 19:21 it was intended to limit punishment, stopping the Jews from going beyond justice. In a nation that was to exemplify justice, unduly severe retribution was replaced by punishment that fitted the crime. Jesus, getting to the heart of the law, goes further still. The people of his kingdom should be prepared not only to demonstrate justice, but to show mercy and even give blessing to the one who wrongs them.

Again and again Jesus shows that, in his kingdom, the law is the bare minimum. To reflect the heart of God is to go deeper. Studying Scripture with this mindset enables us to understand our own relationship to God's law in the light of Jesus' life. If the people of God are going to live the life of the kingdom then external obedience is not enough. In Matthew 5:20 Jesus puts it this way: 'I tell you that unless your righteousness surpasses that of the Pharisees and the teachers of the law, you will certainly not enter the kingdom of heaven.' Unless they allowed it to change their hearts, even the resolute obedience of the Pharisees was not enough.

Unsurprisingly the Pharisees, who considered themselves the most righteous of all Jews, were incensed by statements like this. Matthew 22 records one of the many occasions when they tried to trap Jesus, this time by asking him which commandment was the most important. Jesus answered by quoting Deuteronomy 6:5, 'Love the LORD your God with all your heart and with all your soul and with all your strength', and went on to add the words of Leviticus 19:18, 'love your neighbour as yourself.' When God himself was asked what was at the very heart of the law, his answer was love. We may hear that God is a God of love, but how often have you heard the same said of the law?

The false dichotomy we have created between law and love brought pain to the heart of God long before Jesus voiced it. During another conversation, recorded in Mark 7, Jesus takes God's words in Isaiah and applies them to the Pharisees saying, 'These people honour me with their lips, but their hearts are far from me.'

The first miracle Jesus performed is an indication of the transformation that was taking place. At a wedding in Cana in Galilee Jesus began to display his deity by taking the miraculous and with it transforming a very human problem (John 2:1–8). As the celebrations progressed, disaster struck. Today, running out of wine would be an inconvenience not considered worthy of the dramatic intervention of God. For a Jew at the time of Jesus, to run out of wine at your wedding was social suicide. The resulting stigma would be carried by the young couple for the rest of their lives.

Discovering that the worst had happened, Mary turned to Jesus for help. Even without the evidence of previous miracles, she knew him well enough to believe that anything was possible. At the wedding were six massive stone jars, normally used for ceremonial purification, each one with the capacity to hold twenty to thirty gallons. Jesus instructed the servants to fill them to the brim with water and then draw some out and take it to the master of the feast. As the servant presented this new 'wine' for approval, knowing all too well what was at stake, I imagine he did so with trepidation. Surprisingly, the response was not anger but delight. Not only had the water become wine, it had become the very best wine.

How extraordinary that Jesus would care so deeply for this young couple, intervening in their practical concerns. Sometimes we go so quickly to the spiritual lesson that we miss these moments of absolute humanity. Jesus involved himself in the intimate detail of life, the moment-by-moment living that we so often consider beneath God's notice, and to those moments he brought the heart of God.

You could be forgiven for thinking that I have forgotten what we were talking about. That I have gone off on a tangent and lost my place. What does the wedding in Cana have to do with the law and the Pharisees and love? The answer is: everything.

Alongside meeting a real human need, Jesus was making a point that illustrated what he would later say to the Pharisees. He was giving an object lesson that explained what he would teach in the Sermon on the Mount. Like the water that was used to wash away superficial dirt and make people appear clean, observance of the law could modify external behaviour.

By transforming water into wine, a symbol of inner joy, Jesus was demonstrating a change that went beyond the appearance and penetrated deep into the heart. Obedience on Jesus' terms was not based on external observance, but rooted in the love of God.

It is important not to misunderstand what Jesus was saying. By singling out love for God and for your neighbour as the greatest commandments, he was not minimizing the others. He was not advocating a lifestyle that discarded the law in favour of a feelings-based spirituality. In Matthew 22:40, referring to the commandments to love the Lord your God with all your heart, soul and strength, and love your neighbour as yourself, Jesus says, 'On these two commandments depend the whole Law and the Prophets.' Love is not a new alternative to the law but the standard that underwrites it.

Without love we will never be able to understand, much less live, the law. In fact, when we approach it with hearts that are so unlike the heart of God, our inability to keep the law shows us how far short of his standards we fall. Law without love will end in empty dogma and empty hearts. Similarly, attempts to love God without understanding his character and obeying his law will inevitably be shallow and rocked by feelings and circumstance.

The apostle Paul, author of a large part of the New Testament, started out as a Pharisee. Steeped in the law and determined to obey it to the letter, he considered belief in Jesus to be blasphemy. For him, law without love resulted in hatred so profound that it led him to hunt down and murder the followers of Jesus. When he famously encountered God for himself on the Damascus Road, his thinking was completely reversed. In Romans 13:10, as Paul explains to the believers in Rome the relationship between law and grace, he reminds them that 'love is the fulfilment of the law'. In Jesus, we are finally able to see the law fulfilled and understand the love that is at its heart. For Jews like Paul, as for many people today, viewing the law in this way was a radical change of perspective.

While the words of Jesus are often depicted as gentle and uncontroversial, in their context they were anything but. If the Israelites were physically affected by the voice of God at Sinai, it should not surprise us to discover that the words of Jesus had an equally dramatic effect on those who heard them.

John 6 is most famous for the feeding of the five thousand. In a story that has become so well known, Jesus takes five loaves and two small fish and uses them to feed the huge crowd. Having seen this miracle the people recognize Jesus as the culmination of all they have been waiting for and declare, 'Surely this is the Prophet who is to come into the world' (v. 14). The intention of the people was to make Jesus king forcibly, but instead he slipped away. He knew that their response was based only on their desire to have their physical needs met. The reality of life in God's kingdom is so much more than food on demand. As he went on to explain in graphic terms what it means to follow him, it proved too much for most.

In Deuteronomy 12:23 the Israelites were forbidden to eat meat with blood still in it as, according to Leviticus 17:11, 'the life of a creature is in the blood'. The life represented by the blood of the animal belonged to God alone. In the light of this law, ingrained into the minds of the Jews for centuries, Jesus' explanation of his kingdom is utterly explosive. In words that shock even his disciples, Jesus says, 'unless you eat the flesh of the Son of Man and drink his blood, you have no life in you' (John 6:53).

Jesus was not suggesting some bizarre new ritual, but using powerful imagery to respond to a question that even his own life had not yet answered. It's all very well to say Jesus raised the bar, but how could people who had been unable to keep the law up to this point now live to a standard that was higher still? How could people who had repeatedly rejected him now live as part of his kingdom? With these words Jesus is inviting the people he loves not just to follow him, but to receive his life. Just as God had provided the manna in the wilderness, Jesus himself would be everything they needed to sustain the life they had in him. The God who had given them his law was now giving them himself and inviting them not just to reflect his heart, but to have his heart.

This is love that the human mind cannot contain. That a holy God would call his people to be like him is remarkable. That he would contain his holiness within a human body so that we could see it is awe inspiring. That he would give us his heart and enable us to live in the strength of his own life is more than we can fully comprehend. To make such a thing possible would require the most daring, unparalleled and inconceivable act of love that humanity has ever seen.

Discussion questions

1. Read Matthew 5:17 again. What was Jesus' attitude to the law? In what ways did he fulfil it?
2. How did the teachings of Jesus relate to the law God gave the nation of Israel?
3. Read Matthew 22:34–40. What did Jesus say was the heart of the law? What does this mean? How should this impact our understanding of obedience today?
4. If the law was to be obeyed to a standard higher than even that of the Pharisees, how would that be possible?

14 The death and resurrection of Jesus

Death is crushed to death;
Life is mine to live,
Won through Your selfless love
This the power of the cross
Christ became sin for us
Bore the wrath, paid the cost
We stand forgiven at the cross
(Keith Getty and Stuart Townend)[1]

If Jesus' life was the crescendo of history, then his death silenced even the heavens. How was it possible for God to die? So much of what the Jews had learned through their relationship with God had prepared the world not only for the reality, but for the necessity of this moment.

We know that the words Jesus spoke as he demonstrated the character of God provoked a reaction in those who heard them. Both his words and his actions built on a foundation of

---

1   Extract taken from 'The Power of the Cross' by Keith Getty and Stuart Townend copyright © 2005 Thankyou Music.

Old Testament knowledge that his Jewish listeners had been devoted to from childhood. In just a passing reference Jesus was able to say things that are easily missed by ears less tuned to the Hebrew Bible. When he rode into Jerusalem on a donkey, he not only echoed King Solomon's coronation in I Kings I, but openly fulfilled the prophecy of Zechariah who said, 'See, your king comes to you, righteous and having salvation, gentle and riding on a donkey' (Zechariah 9:9). As he passed them, with the fragrance of Mary's anointing oil still clinging to his hair and body, the Jews knew exactly what he was saying. Their true King had finally come.

Jesus' claim to kingship was not an attempt to overthrow the rulers of the day or physically sit on the throne of Israel, but a reminder that a new kingdom had arrived. A kingdom that was above human rulers or geography and whose king was God himself. While some saw what he was and rejoiced in it, Israel, as a nation, rejected him once more. In an act of rebellion that demonstrated the depths of evil in the human heart, they set in motion a plan to kill the God who had always loved them. The betrayal that began in Eden, and culminated in a garden outside Jerusalem, was fronted on that night by a man who had been one of Jesus' closest friends. Unable to accept a God who did not fit his own preconceptions, Judas led the party that came to take the life of Jesus.

There is a beautiful moment in the darkness of the garden which reveals events from a different perspective entirely. Knowing everything that was about to happen, Jesus got up and went out to meet his betrayers. Even the conversation that followed was instigated by him as he asked, 'Who are you looking for?' When they reply, 'Jesus of Nazareth', and he answers, 'I am he', something happens that I skipped over for years without noticing. John 18:6 tells us that at the sound of his voice the soldiers, with their armour and weapons and bravado, fell to the ground. Once again they were shown that this was their God, before whom they were powerless, and we are reminded that even in his final hours, he was the one in control. As they lay there on the ground, his was the voice that urged them to stand. In a mind-blowing demonstration of his love for his people even at their very worst, the one who could have ended their lives in a heartbeat lifted them back to their feet and allowed them to continue. As Jesus was seized and dragged off to a mock trial most of his followers ran away. This was a battle that only God himself could fight. With monumental restraint, the power of God was held back as Jesus allowed the people he loved to physically turn their hatred on him.

In the hours that followed, the people who were afraid to speak the name of God out of respect for his absolute holiness looked into his face and mocked him. Soldiers whose legs had given way at the sound of his voice now slapped and beat him until his blood ran onto the ground and his face was barely recognizable. Mouths that should have been silenced forever by his glory left spittle running down his beard. The high king of heaven allowed men to take a crown of thorns and drive it into his skull in a barbaric mockery of all that he is.

After all this the people were given an opportunity to release Jesus. In words that rang with more truth than he could ever comprehend, Pilate stood the battered form of Jesus before them and asked, 'Shall I crucify your King?' What was the response of the people of God, the nation chosen to live as he led and enjoy all that he had offered them? The chief priests, the men charged with the responsibility of bringing the nation into the presence of God, replied on behalf of the people, 'We have no king but Caesar' (John 19:15).

Just as I clung to the hope that I would have stood with men like Joshua, I believed for a long time that I would not have betrayed Jesus. One night, several years ago, I realized with startling clarity how very wrong I was. I was at a play staged in an old warehouse in Belfast. It was an unusual production with focal points at various places around the huge space. Rather than sitting down, the audience were required to move around with the action. As far as I know the actors were not Christians. They told the story of Jesus' death simply for its theatrical appeal. The emotionally charged scenes with Pilate were staged at one end. When they were finished the actor playing Jesus was dragged the considerable distance to the opposite side of the warehouse, where the scene was set for the crucifixion. As was intended, I began to follow with the rest of the audience. Dotted among us as we walked were several of the actors and, as the group pushed its way towards the crucifixion scene, they began to shout, 'Crucify him'. I will never forget the moment the chant was taken up. Without warning I found myself powerless against the wave of people who pushed forward to see what would happen. Deafened by the shouts and pulled in every direction I simply let the momentum carry me along. Without uttering a word I was part of the crowd. In that moment I knew how easily I could have joined the angry mob who followed Jesus to the cross. The realization moved me to tears.

In our comfortable twenty-first-century world we seem far removed from the crowd that hounded Jesus to his death. The truth is, the chant that came from hearts that had rejected God has echoed deep in each of us. In recognizing this we find ourselves among the people who took Jesus outside the city and drove nails through his hands and feet and left him on a cross to die. To think in these terms does not make for comfortable reading. In fact, it uncovers a part of us we try our best to hide. Yet unless we realize how closely we are tied to the rebels who crucified Jesus, unless we realize where we stand before God, it is impossible to grasp the importance of that night in Jerusalem.

It is not possible for the human mind to comprehend fully the enormity of what took place when God hung on a Roman cross. Having said that, the Bible is full of pictures and insights that can help deepen our understanding of the hours that changed our relationship with him forever.

Death on a cross was a brutal, undignified, humiliating and excruciatingly painful way to end your life. The Romans were experts in inflicting suffering and crucifixion was designed as a graphic and effective deterrent for anyone who would consider going against the authority of Rome. It was a punishment to be avoided at all costs and certainly not one that anyone would choose to undergo. To choose the cross was to knowingly put yourself through one of the worst forms of torture that the human body can endure. Yet Jesus did. I have often wondered why he didn't choose a less brutal death, or come at a time when execution was more humane. I'm sure there are theological reasons which we could debate but I sometimes wonder if he chose it because, in the physical agony of the cross, we have a picture of a spiritual agony we will never comprehend. It shows us the agony endured by a holy God when he became sin in all its depravity.

During the hours before Jesus finally died the earth was plunged into darkness. For the first and only time the relationship between Jesus and his father was severed and he cried out in the pain of an abandonment that mankind need never feel. The God who promised never to leave his people was forced to turn his back on his own son. Do you remember the curse that Moses told the Israelites would come with disobedience? The death and separation from God that would be the inevitable consequence of their choice to go their own way? Paul explains in Galatians 3:13 that Jesus became that curse for us.

The God whose holiness could not overlook our sin, yet whose love would not allow him to turn away from us, did the only thing possible. Such was the love of God that he took the full force of his anger towards sin and turned it on himself. In those three hours he felt the pain of every thought, every word, every action and every choice that mankind has made in rebellion against him. The shame that you feel in your worst moments, and the evil that has ravaged humanity for centuries, were all laid on Jesus. All the rebellion of centuries past, as well as those still to come, were placed on him as he stood, cloaked in darkness, where we should have been.

I heard a story that helps to illustrate one aspect of what Jesus did for us. Years ago in America as a group of pioneers made their way to their new home, they were horrified to notice a plume of smoke coming rapidly towards them. The dry grass was burning rapidly and they knew they could not outrun the fire that was about to overtake them. One of their leaders told them to burn the area of grass behind them and, when the flames subsided, the whole group stood in the middle of the burnt piece of ground. As the fire roared towards them a little girl cried out in terror, 'Are you sure we shall not all be burned up?' The leader replied, 'My child, the flames cannot reach us here, for we are standing where the fire has been!' When Jesus felt the full force of God's judgment on sin he absorbed it completely. When we stand with him we stand where judgment has already fallen and it will not fall again.

It was no coincidence that Jesus' death occurred when the Jewish people were celebrating the Passover. As they remembered the time when God had set them free from Egypt, a lamb was once again taking their place. Jews who had watched the death of many lambs knew what it meant to rely on the sacrifice that was made on their behalf. The powerful picture helped explain the reality of what happened when Jesus died.

Jesus is described in Scripture not only as the lamb, but as the high priest. On the Day of Atonement, when the high priest brought the sacrifice for the people he did it dressed in intricate robes designed by God himself. The robes reminded both the priest and the people that no-one could stand in the presence of God without protection. When Jesus came into the presence of God on our behalf, not only bringing the sacrifice, but as the sacrifice itself, there were no such robes. In contrast to the priests he was naked, disfigured and totally unprotected from the judgment of God.

Every moment of guilt you have ever felt was experienced by God in those hours. There is nothing left that he has not seen and nothing that he has not dealt with. As you grasp that truth the initial horror and shame of it is replaced by a freedom that cannot be matched. When everything is stripped away and the reality of all that we are in the depths of our being is laid bare, we long to be accepted. How ironic that we find that acceptance only in the presence of the God who demands absolute holiness. Why? Because he has not only seen all that we are but he has suffered for it and yet his love for us remains unchanged. He not only accepts us for who we are but he offers us the chance to be all that we were meant to be. That is true freedom.

At the end of those hours of darkness Jesus finally died. The soldiers could no more have killed him than they could give themselves life. Yet, in a way that is hard for us to grasp, Jesus gave up his life and submitted to death. As he did so he spoke three words that brought hope to the hearts of men. 'It is finished' (John 19:30). In those three words he brought to an end the whole sacrificial system. No longer would the sacrifice of animals be required. Never again would the high priest have to come trembling into the Holy of Holies with the blood of a lamb. The sacrifice was over and the price had been paid. A new covenant had been made.

The covenant God made with his people on Sinai was based on their obedience. The covenant he made on the cross was also based on obedience, but this time it was the perfect obedience of Jesus who did what we could never do. Traditionally, when a covenant was made, the two parties would exchange robes. At the cross Jesus took our rags and dressed us instead in the holiness that allowed us to enter his presence.

In the moment Jesus died something happened in the temple that demonstrated the monumental change which had just occurred. The Holy of Holies, the place representing the very presence of God, was protected by a thick curtain that veiled his holiness. At the moment Jesus died the veil was ripped in two from top to bottom, not by human hands but by God himself. I often try to picture the reaction of the priests when they realized the veil had been torn. Terror must have given way to shock as they realized they were still alive. As the message spread, the ripples of astonished murmurs must have grown into shouts that echoed round the temple and out into the city.

For the first time, anyone, no matter who they were, could have access to the presence of God. The tragedy is that the Jews as a people continued as though nothing had happened. They put up barriers to God that no longer needed to be there. All too often we follow suit. We consider ourselves or others unworthy of God's presence. We try to smarten ourselves up or lay down requirements for those who want to approach him. To do that is to limit the freedom for which Jesus sacrificed his life.

Because of the cross, the only thing we need to come to God, who has spent history declaring his love, is Jesus himself.

Because of what he did we can enter into a new covenant with him that is symbolized by the idea of walking through the torn veil. When Jesus walked on earth the veil that contained the holiness of God was his human body and when that body was broken on the cross a path opened into the presence of God. In order to enter into this new covenant, this new relationship with God himself, we simply have to accept what Jesus did for us. Intentionally stepping into the covenant he offers us, we can leave behind the lives that have been marked by rebellion. When we take that step, we will discover it is just the first in a journey that our lives will not complete. John, as he wrote his gospel, explained why he was recording all the signs that Jesus performed, including his death and resurrection. He wrote, 'these are written that you may believe that Jesus is the Christ, the Son of God, and that by believing you may have life in his name' (John 20:31).

The belief that John talks about is not mental agreement, but complete reliance on all that Jesus is and all that he has done. Like the choice facing the Israelites on the plains of Moab, this is not a one-off decision. It is not a one-night stand with God or a momentary transaction securing a ticket which can simply be saved for some future event. Belief, in these terms, is a life-changing commitment to place our lives under the authority of the God who knows us better than we know ourselves. It is willingly taking our place in the kingdom that has him at the head.

If the story ended with the death of Jesus it would be a noble story but one that changed nothing. If death could overpower God then we have no hope. The good news is that when Mary and then the disciples went to visit the grave of Jesus, they found it empty. The death that would have crushed us was no match for God himself. The impact of the resurrection of Jesus was seen as the group of men who had abandoned him were transformed into followers who stood for him with their last breath.

As Jesus appeared to his disciples and others after his resurrection, they began to grasp the reality of all that God had been teaching them all along. Not just in the life of Jesus, but through all the history that had led up to that point. Just as the exodus freed the Israelites from slavery and set them on the path to the inheritance they had been promised, Jesus' death and resurrection freed his people and invited them to take their place in his kingdom. As God had always intended, his kingdom would now be open to anyone who came to him on the basis of what Jesus had done. Those people would now be his witnesses in all the world.

Before he finally returned to heaven, Jesus told his disciples to wait in Jerusalem until they were 'clothed with power from on high' (Luke 24:49). Fifty days after Jesus' death his disciples were celebrating the Feast of Pentecost. As they commemorated the moment fifty days after the exodus, when God descended on Sinai, they experienced his presence again. This time the fire did not come down on a mountain or even on the temple, but on the disciples themselves. The dwelling of God was now in his people. By the presence of the Holy Spirit within them, God would enable the people of this new kingdom to live in the obedience to which they had always been called, with the joy that came only in his presence.

Discussion questions

1. What was the response of mankind to the presence of their God? Why? How do verses like John 18:6 help us understand what was really happening?

2. Read 2 Corinthians 5:21. How did God deal with the inevitable consequences of disobedience? What is his acceptance of us now based entirely upon?

3. Read John 3:16 and 20:31. If belief in Jesus goes beyond mental agreement, what does it actually mean? What is the life that we can have in his name? What is the alternative?

4. If God dwelt on earth first in the tabernacle, then the temple and then in the human body of Jesus, where is his dwelling on earth now? How should this affect our ability to live as God intended?

15 Walking worthy

I urge you to live a life worthy of the
calling you have received.
(Ephesians 4:1)

As the story of what God had done began to spread, even in the face of fierce opposition, it was unstoppable. The book of Acts chronicles the birth of the early church, as men and women, now equipped and led by the Holy Spirit, began to live lives that were evidence of the power of God within them. Through Jesus, God not only provided a way into his presence for the nation of Israel, he now extended that invitation to those who for so long had been watching from the sidelines. The rescue that began in the Jewish nation filtered out until even the Gentiles (non-Jews) discovered that life as God intended could be theirs.

Paul's letter to the Ephesians is written to a local church made up predominantly of these new believers. Logically, and with contagious joy, Paul helps the Ephesians grasp and understand the position they find themselves in before God. Then, in the light of this truth, he sets before them the importance of living lives that are worthy of their great God, not only individually, but together in unity.

Just as Moses began his reading of the law by reminding God's people of their story, Paul begins by reminding the Ephesians of all that God has done for them and who they now are in him. From the beginning he makes it clear that including the Gentiles in the kingdom of God was not plan B. It was not an attempt to rectify a situation that had gone wrong. They were never God's second choice. As he had always intended, all God's people could now call him Father in a way even the nation of Israel could not previously have imagined.

Jew or Gentile, the grace offered at the cross is beautifully illustrated in the parable of the prodigal son. After rebelling, turning his back on his father and rejecting the life that could have been his, the son heads out to make his own way in the world. Inevitably, when his money runs out he ends up lonely, hungry and hopeless. Unknown to him, through it all his father has been waiting and watching. When the day comes that the son decides to go home and ask for forgiveness, his father's response is beyond anything he could have imagined. Setting aside his dignity the father hitches up his cloak and runs to him with open arms. A boy whose actions by law were deserving of death was wrapped instead in his father's robe and welcomed back as a treasured son.

From the moment mankind first chose to turn their back on him, God had been preparing a way for them to come back home. The forgiveness God offers goes beyond what we could ever have hoped for. In Jesus we have been freely given what we could never have deserved. In the words of Paul in Ephesians 1:7–8, God has 'lavished' on us the 'riches of his grace', giving us an inheritance fitting for sons of the Most High God. Throwing his robe around us, he welcomes us into his family. Sealed by the presence of the Holy Spirit, our place as his children is secured forever. Our inheritance is guaranteed.

As the list of blessings grows, layer upon layer as the letter progresses, Paul reminds the Ephesians of the change that has already taken place. Even when they turned their backs to God, he, with a love that was not altered by their sin, stepped in and transformed everything. People who were once dead were made alive in Christ. Men and women without hope discovered that he had created them for a purpose. Those who were once strangers to God became fellow citizens and members of God's household with all the privileges afforded to their position as sons. Individuals who were once alone were now part of a big story.

Whether they are Jews or Gentiles, the position the believers now find themselves in is theirs purely because of what Jesus accomplished on their behalf. They cannot earn it or lose it. Their circumstances cannot change it. As they stand, drenched in what Paul describes as the 'unfathomable riches of Christ' (Ephesians 3:8), how should the people of God respond?

The answer to that question is as crucial today as it was for the early church. While 2,000 years may have passed, in practical terms the position we find ourselves in before God is the same as that of the Ephesians. We are no longer faced with the curse that came from disobedience to the law of God. In Jesus that debt was fully paid. Not only are we free, but we now have the life of God within us in the form of the Holy Spirit, enabling us to live as God intended. Just as the Ephesians' new-found freedom required a response, our understanding of this indescribable gift must not be limited to theory.

Having laid before them the reality of their relationship with a holy God and the extravagance of his love towards them, Paul turns to practical life, urging the Ephesians to live lives that are worthy of the calling they have received

(Ephesians 4:1). As they allow God to renew their minds through his word and in the power of the Holy Spirit, they are to respond by walking in love, imitating the life of Jesus. Every move they make must be consistent with the character of the God who has called them his. Just as Moses called the Israelites to reflect the holiness of God and embody his character, Paul writes to the Ephesians urging them to live lives that demonstrate the heart of the kingdom of which they are now a part.

In Ephesians 4, Paul makes it clear that even speech was to be governed by the holiness of God. The lies, anger, bitterness and slander which were in evidence around them were to have no place in the lives of God's people. Instead, every word coming out of their mouths was to reflect the presence of the Holy Spirit within. Equally, today, it is impossible to embrace one kingdom with our hearts while reflecting another with our mouths. Whether it is in our humour, our on-line comments or even our casual conversations, holiness must translate to speech.

In marriage, both husbands and wives were to demonstrate faithfulness, treating one another in a way that was consistent with the character of their God. He was to be honoured in their homes, with children obeying their parents even when society, peer pressure and hormones were pushing them in the opposite direction. Parents were not to exasperate their children, instead bringing them up in the training and instruction of the Lord. In the workplace, both slave and master were to work to the best of their ability, taking every opportunity to display the heart of God.

Perhaps it should not surprise us that this picture of God's kingdom sounds familiar. If his heart remains constant, then the life that reflects it will not change either. Rather than changing its content, Paul's words to the Ephesians simply put God's call to his people on the plains of Moab into context within a new chapter of the same story.

When Moses urged the nation of Israel to choose life, their position as the people of God was not in question. What was at stake was the intimacy of their walk with God, their effectiveness in the role they had been given and their enjoyment of all that was theirs in him. By choosing obedience to the life God showed them in the law, they could choose to live as God intended.

For us, to choose life is consciously to put on the new self, the new man or woman created in the holiness of God and dressed in the righteousness of Christ. While our position before God cannot be altered, our intimacy with him, our effectiveness as his people and our enjoyment of all he has given us are very much at stake.

Paul not only urges the Ephesians to live lives that are worthy of their calling, he stresses the importance of doing so together. In a world that has become obsessed with the individual, concerned only with what I want and what I need, Paul's words are a much-needed reminder to the people of God that we are part of a bigger picture.

We have one God whose character is unchanging. We have one Lord who secured our freedom with his own life. We come to him on the basis of one faith that is unaltered by circumstance, personality or background. We are one body with many parts. We are indwelt by one Spirit and we are called with one calling. What we are, we are together.

Unity is an indispensable part of our calling as the people of God, yet for the church in Ephesus it was not an easy task. Centuries of segregation between Jews and Gentiles had led to deep-seated resentment that would not easily be set aside. Two groups with different backgrounds, different cultures and different experiences of God now had to learn to serve him together as one. When Paul calls the Ephesians to exercise humility and patience with each other, this is not a small request. Human affection alone would not enable them to show the love that was consistent with their life in Christ. To love on God's terms would require them to live intentionally out of the overflow of the love that he had placed within their hearts.

Interestingly, as Paul challenges the Ephesians to live out their calling he urges them to *preserve* the unity they have been given. They are not to create or manufacture it but to maintain something that is already there. Given as a gift from God, the unity to which they were called was greater than all the differences that had previously separated them. The choice the Ephesians faced was whether they would keep this supernatural unity, or allow it to be destroyed by their natural differences. As the church of God today, we face the same choice and the decision we make has massive implications when it comes to fulfilling the privileged role God has given us. In holding on to the unity that defied their immediate instincts, the church in Ephesus would powerfully demonstrate to their community the change that had taken place in their lives. Similarly, when we live out our call to unity, evangelism becomes less about convincing people we are different and more about answering the questions that arise when they see the difference for themselves.

It was the impact of this kind of unity that moved Jesus to pray for the church even as he prepared to face the cross. In John 17, Jesus prays not only for his followers, but also for those who would eventually believe in him. In his final hours, you and I were on the heart of Jesus. It was his prayer that we would experience the same unity that exists between himself and God the Father. As they are completely one, inseparable, part of a relationship that is perfect love, so we are to be with one another. Unity is so integral to the life of the kingdom that Jesus says in John 13:35, 'By this all men will know that you are my disciples, if you love one another.' According to Jesus, if we do not show this love for one another the world around us has every right to conclude that we are not his disciples.

What a phenomenal responsibility! It is unsurprising that Paul urges the Ephesians to be *diligent* in preserving their unity. While it is a gift from God, this kind of unity cannot be maintained without intentional and often sacrificial action. If we are to be unified, there will be times when we will not get our own way. Sometimes the faults of another may have to go unpunished and our egos will have to be overruled. Practical unity is a hard road, with painful knocks along the way, but it is the only road open to those who want to play their part in God's story.

As well as being an outward demonstration of God's love itself, when we learn to see one another through God's eyes there are enormous blessings to be gained from people with a different outlook on life. In Ephesus, Jews who had grown up immersed in the law gained a fresh perspective from Gentiles, who perhaps understood on a deeper level that the gift they had been given could not be earned. On the other hand, Gentiles who understood their freedom had much to learn from their Jewish brothers about the holiness and obedience which were a fitting response to his love.

Within my local church and wider Christian family, there are people who are different from me in almost every way. From a teenage boy who refuses to compromise his faith, whatever challenges may come his way, to a ninety-four-year-old grandmother whose failing eyesight and faltering steps do nothing to hinder the joy born from a lifetime of steadfast faith. From a young mother with little schooling but a deep understanding of God's heart, to a lawyer who uses his sharp mind to study and teach the Scriptures. All of these people, and many more, have brought a new dimension to my understanding of God. Whether because of age, background or even just personality, if it was not for our common bond in Christ it is probable that our paths would never have crossed. Ironically it has often been those same friends, with an outlook so different from my own, who have pulled me back when I have been in danger of falling between the gaps in my own understanding. Within the church as a whole, as well as in our own local representation of it, there is a wealth of experience from which we can benefit.

One of the greatest barriers to unity is the fact that we confuse unity with uniformity. While unity is written on the heart of God, uniformity has never been part of his plan. With the creativity that is inherent in his nature God made species of birds and fish and insect so numerous that many are yet to be discovered. From the great African elephant to the tiny neon fish that dart among the coral, nature teems with a diversity that brings joy to the heart of God. Why do we assume that when this same God calls people to join his kingdom he will make them all identical?

Within the kingdom of God is a spectrum of personality, appearance, talent and quirkiness that can only make you smile. From the mathematician to the street artist, from those who control vast business empires to travellers who own only the clothes on their back, God's people are as diverse as they are loved. When we come to God his desire is not to turn us into religious clones but to transform us into the very best version of ourselves.

God is so vast, so beyond our understanding, that to suggest any one person could reflect his nature in its entirety is nonsense. While our local churches may reflect different approaches to structure or public worship, it is important that our understanding of unity is not confined to those same groups. The nation of Israel was organized into twelve tribes and Moses' blessing at the end of Deuteronomy reflects different characteristics of each. The problem that divided Israel began not when they reflected God in their unique way, but when they tried to create a God who suited their own purposes. When we reduce our understanding of him to our own experience our lives stop being about the reflection of his glory, becoming instead an attempt to define God in terms of our own personality.

As a student, I was determined to try new things and so when a friend asked me to join the Gilbert and Sullivan Society I immediately agreed. I have to confess that I had very little idea who Gilbert and Sullivan were. I had certainly never taken part in an operetta. As we rehearsed for the production we were divided into groups according to our vocal range and, with my limited musical ability, I tried to master the part I had been given. It was not until the first time we sang all the parts together that I realized the importance of learning my own. As the different notes blended the result was beautiful and, inspired by the music that filled the room, I sang my lines with all my heart. The song we sang was the same but as we sang in harmony we revealed a richness that I could never have discovered on my own.

As we each reflect something of God's nature, in the way he has designed us, our collective harmonies will better reveal the splendour of who he is. Whether it is in the teacher who cares for the minds of each new generation or the artist who somehow captures the beauty of a sunset, God is glorified. His care is evident in the medics who use their skill to bring healing to damaged bodies and in the farmers who work the land to provide food for a hungry world. His heart can be seen in those who bring aid to people devastated by natural disaster and in accountants who try to bring a sense of order to financial crisis. Each of us, in our daily lives, are given opportunities to display something of the character of God, painting together a much bigger picture of his heart than any one of us could ever do alone.

Such potential comes with responsibility. If we refuse to learn our part, or even worse ambush or belittle the role God has given someone else, we obscure the church's reflection of God. If we are to allow our unique personality to be a reflection of his character then we have to know him, obey him and allow him to teach us the part we were created to play. In submitting ourselves to the truth we find within his word we discover that, rather than being restricted, we are freed to properly experience beauty that will make our hearts sing.

Despite my enthusiasm, I have to confess that there were many times I hit notes neither Gilbert nor Sullivan had ever intended. In each departure from the score I caused a jarring discord that was all too evident. When I made up my own tune, the notes which were meant to complement each other clashed. The beauty of the music was spoiled.

The reality is that your role in the kingdom of God is important and, while that is an awesome privilege, your failure to fulfil it will impoverish the people of God. Let me be clear that my intention is not to cause you to feel fear or guilt. I have fallen short of God's standards more times than I care to remember and I am grateful that our failures cannot diminish God's love any more than our successes can enhance it. Rather, my intention is to encourage you to take seriously the awesome privilege you have as part of the family of God. Our call to unity goes beyond patience with each other and forgiveness for the times we fall short, however hard that may be. Unity in the body of Christ involves making sure we are living the lives to which we have been called, in a way that preserves our collective reflection of the heart of God. When we use our gifts to strengthen the church we are able collectively to stand firm in a world that will otherwise pull us in every direction.

In our diversity we are called to have the heart of the same God, living lives marked by obedience to him. As people are drawn to love that cannot be rationally explained, we will begin to understand why our unity was on the heart of Jesus as he prepared to make it possible. We are part of a battle that makes anything else look tame in comparison. It is a battle we cannot win unless we stand together.

In Matthew 16:18 Jesus says to Peter, 'I will build my church and the gates of hell will not prevail against it' (NASB). Until recently I thought those words meant I was simply protected against the kingdom of darkness, that when Jesus destroyed death he rendered it impotent against those who were secure in him. While that is absolutely and wonderfully true there is much more to his statement.

When was the last time you were attacked by a gate? Unless you have a particularly unusual story to tell, the answer is probably never. Rather than to attack, the role of a gate is to defend property. When we move forward together, in the armour God has provided, the powers of darkness are defenceless against us. We are called to go out in God's strength and live lives that are marked by his love and worthy of his kingdom, proclaiming his heart to a world in need of rescue. Evangelism is not about shouting condemnation at people who are already struggling with lives that are out of control. If we are to convince those around us that God loves them, we have to start by demonstrating that love ourselves. If we want the people we love to know that God can transform their lives, we can begin by allowing God to transform ours.

In 1 Peter 3:15, as Peter passed on the lessons he had learned from Jesus, he urged the believers to 'always be prepared to give an answer to everyone who asks you to give the reason for the hope that you have'. When did someone last ask you to explain the difference that is evident in your life?

If we are going to have an opportunity to give an answer, our lives must first raise a question. In a world that finds itself increasingly in despair, a life marked by hope will shine like a beacon. While the outcome of the epic war between two kingdoms was determined by Jesus on the cross, the battle for the hearts of individuals rages all around us. If we want to play our part in the big story we will not do it with anger, arrogance or condemnation but with love, obedience and holiness as we, individually and collectively, go out into our schools, businesses, homes and communities and live like we belong to the Most High God.

Discussion questions

1. Read Ephesians 1. What are some of the blessings that are ours if we are in Christ? How would it impact our everyday lives if we lived with a deep awareness of these truths?
2. What does it mean, practically, to live a life worthy of the calling we have received? (Ephesians 4:1)
3. What is the difference between unity and uniformity? How can the church be enhanced by the diversity of its members? In practical terms, what does it mean to maintain unity in diversity?
4. Read John 13:34–35. What was Jesus teaching the disciples? How does our disunity affect our collective ability to reflect the character of God?

16 Joining the Haverim

The people who know their God
will display strength and take action.
(Daniel 11:32b NASB)

If you were to open this book and tell me you had time to read only one chapter, I would direct you here. This chapter is not better written, nor are the contents of the others less important. I would tell you to read it because if you grasp the importance of knowing God's word you will discover the rest for yourself. At best, what I say may spark your interest, or encourage you to go deeper. What God says to you directly will shake your world and leave you longing for more. What I have discovered in the pages of Scripture has changed me more than all the sermons I have ever heard and all the books I have ever read. If you really want to know your God, the place to start is in his word.

A couple of years ago I decided to plant some flowers in pots around our garden. Ellie and Lara were very small at the time and so I thought it wise to leave the plants in the back of my car until the girls were asleep. During the day I had prepared the soil in the pots and then left them in the garden while Ellie and her friend played. All went according to plan and that night I added the flowers to the pots and went to bed pleased with my efforts. The next morning as I prepared breakfast I heard words that always cause me alarm: 'Mummy, Mummy, come quick. You have to see what's happened!' Running out to the garden I found Ellie jumping up and down with excitement. With eyes like saucers she gestured wildly at the flowers and said, 'Last night Sophie and I planted raisins and stones and look what has happened!'

This is very often our approach to God's word. A sermon here, a Christian book there, the odd home group and a thought for the day when we remember. Taking whatever happens to come our way we expect to grow into mature Christians who carry the image of their God. I wanted flowers that would bring colour to my garden. I didn't get them by planting bits and pieces I found on the path. If I want to know God then I have to begin by developing a solid understanding of his word. To do that I must intentionally study the Scriptures through which he has revealed himself.

If I want to know God, I must cultivate an understanding of him that is based on Scripture as a whole, not simply on selected passages. Paul, in Romans 15:4, reminds the believers of the continuing importance of what we know as the Old Testament, saying, 'for everything that was written in the past was written to teach us, so that through endurance and the encouragement of the Scriptures we might have hope.' In John 8:31–32, Jesus urges his disciples to hold fast to all that he has taught them. He says, 'if you hold to my teaching, you are really my disciples. Then you will know the truth, and the truth will set you free.' To follow Jesus is to become part of a kingdom people who have always been people of his word, whether that word was given first to the nation of Israel as they prepared to enter the Promised Land, or to the early church as an explanation of life in the new covenant. If we are going to stand as the people of God we need to know who he is. In a sobering reminder of the consequences of neglecting his word, God says in Hosea 4:6, 'my people are destroyed from lack of knowledge.' It is impossible to grow into the people we were created to be and live in the hope of who we are in him, without knowing his word.

Never before has there been such a wealth of material available to help us study the Bible. Books, study guides, CDs, conferences and so much more bombard us with tips for study, yet generally speaking, our understanding of God's word remains so limited. Why is this the case?

With so much to compete for our attention, and so many other things that require less effort, we discover we have to use a tool that has fallen badly out of favour: discipline. In our modern world the commitment it takes to get to know God jars with our need for instant satisfaction. I have often wished someone would invent spiritual jump-leads, that somehow I could plug myself into the people I most admire and download the lifetime of knowledge they have accumulated.

No matter what you are told, there is no short cut to studying the Bible. Knowing God is a lifelong commitment that requires hard decisions. It involves setting aside times when you turn off the television or computer and unplug the phone. It involves getting up when you would rather hit snooze.

Some time ago I had the opportunity to meet the man through whom my mother became a Christian as a child. He was speaking on 'Encountering God in His Word' and, as he began, I was expecting a long list of tools, gleaned from years of faithful service, which would help me in my own studies. I was wrong. With a gentleness that brought authenticity to his words he said, 'Everyone is as close to God as they want to be.' Can that really be true? Am I the only thing stopping me from being closer to God? As I began to think about my own life, I realized how often the seemingly unimportant choices I make reflect the desires of my heart.

It is so much easier to believe that God will draw close to me on my terms. That if I find five minutes after my lie-in, he will be there. That he will be thrilled if I squeeze him into the break between my favourite TV programmes. That even though I devoted years to my education it is OK to give the Bible just a passing glance at bedtime. That it is fine to work such long hours that there is no time or energy left for him. The problem is that he understands fully. He understands that when I say I love him, the place I give him in my life betrays my words. He knows when I say I want to put him first, I mean first after all the things that matter more.

Am I as close to God as I want to be? What if I was to make time for his word a priority, fitting other things in around him instead of the other way around? How would my life change? Would I miss out or would the rewards be greater than the sacrifices I had made? The discipline it takes to study God's word is an ongoing battle that has to be fought day after day, but the time and effort involved are far outweighed by the joy to be discovered along the way. If I really believe I could ever lose out by putting God first, I have completely misunderstood the heart of a God who longs to bless his children.

Perhaps another reason we minimize the importance of intentional study is a misunderstanding of the role of the Holy Spirit. Some time ago there was a young pilot who had been preparing long and hard for his first solo flight. He pored over the manuals for hours, making sure he understood every word and committing the contents to memory. Finally the big day came. The weather was perfect for the hour-long flight.

Take-off went without a hitch, as did the first part of the flight. About thirty minutes later the weather changed. Almost instantly, the young pilot found himself in dense fog with no visibility at all. Radioing ahead he explained his situation and the air traffic controller agreed to talk him through the landing. As he listened to the voice in his ear and applied it to the knowledge he had already acquired, the pilot was able to bring the plane safely in to land.

The Holy Spirit enables us to obey the word of God, but we cannot obey what we do not know. When we open our Bibles and begin to study, coming first to God and asking him to reveal himself through his word, he will do so. Not only will he change our hearts but he will show us how to apply the truth we discover to the reality of life.

I have found that my promises to put God's word first can be easily made and just as easily broken. When I come across passages I struggle to understand, I can begin to lose heart. Left to my own devices, my commitment to studying the Bible can quickly fade away. Because I find the discipline required to study God's word difficult, I have found the Jewish concept of Haverim invaluable.

Common in the days of Jesus, Haverim were groups of young men who spent their spare time studying and debating the law in an attempt to understand and apply it to life.[1] I am privileged to have a group of women in my life who I count as my 'Haverim'. Using the same materials in our private study, we meet together for an hour every two weeks and discuss what we have learned. Knowing that we will meet together, I find it easier to study alone. When God shows me something exciting, I look forward to sharing it with them. When I struggle to understand a difficult concept, I know that talking it through with them will help me see the truth more clearly.

We do not always agree. I have probably learned most as we debated the things we understood differently. On more than one occasion I have realized that the point of view I argued, with so much determination, was entirely wrong. One thing we have discovered is that it is possible to use our differences of opinion to lead us into a deeper understanding of Scripture rather than to divide us. However, this will only happen if our discussions are born out of our own time in the presence of God. If we are not prayerfully committed to God's word on our own, we end up with clashing personalities and opinions rather than the discovery of truth. In order to bring something meaningful to the group it is vital that I have studied on my own. On the other hand, in order to fully appreciate and explore what I have learned I discuss it with my Haverim.

If it is your desire to get to know God, can I encourage you to try to find another person, or even a group, to study with you? If a group does not already exist, ask God to lead you to someone with whom you could begin to study. As you choose materials to use, make sure they are leading you to study the Bible in context for yourself, rather than telling you what someone else believes and backing it up with isolated verses.[2]

There is a difference between knowing about God and knowing God. Unless we commit ourselves to studying and applying his word we will never know him in the way that he intends. Only when we know him intimately and personally, allowing our minds and hearts to become saturated with his character, will we begin to understand what holiness is.

If you want to love God's word but are struggling to get excited about it, could I make a suggestion? Study it anyway. The love that you are lacking is born in the journey of discovery that takes us deeper into the great story of a great God. Like so many before you, if you choose to persevere and make

God's word a priority, you will find yourself falling in love with him in a way you never expected. Your life will be transformed as you discover for yourself the love that is the heartbeat of his kingdom. Like the restless child who takes their first sip of water on a hot summer's day, you will discover that he is what you have been longing for all along.

Discussion questions

1. Do you agree that everyone is as close to God as they want to be? Why or why not? To what extent do our actions and choices affect our intimacy with God?

2. In Hosea 4:6 God says that his people are 'destroyed from lack of knowledge'. How will ignorance of God's word impact (a) our understanding of who God is, (b) our relationship with him and (c) our ability to live as he intended?

3. Read 2 Timothy 2:15. What is the responsibility of the believer in relation to God's word? How does our handling of God's word relate to the role of the Holy Spirit in our lives?

4. What are the benefits of studying with others who are committed to the word of God? What are the responsibilities of the individual, in order to maximize the effectiveness of group study? If you are not already part of such a group, what steps could you take to join or form one?

17 For such a time as this

Feel the beat of a distant thunder
It's the sound of an ancient song
This is the Kingdom calling
Come now and tread the dawn
Come to the Father
Come to the deeper well
Drink of the water
And come to live a tale to tell
Pages are turning now
This is abundant life
The joy in the journey
Is enough to make a grown man cry
With a little boy heart alive.
(Andrew Peterson)[1]

We began our journey together with a question and we will end with another.

If this story is true, what does it mean to you?

If it is not true, then humanity is lost and there is nothing for it but to make the best of a bad situation. If there is no big story then we must resign ourselves to the fact that dreams are just the product of our overactive imaginations. But if it is true, and I believe with every fibre of my being that it is, then we are faced with a possibility that will cause even the darkest heart to sing.

If it is true, then the glimpses of his story which crop up again and again in our movies and books and songs are simply another reminder that our hearts have always been, and always will be, meant for him.

In the movie *Avatar*, I was particularly struck by the moment when Jake Sully, a wounded marine whose injuries left him confined to a wheelchair, not only regains the use of his legs, but learns how to fly. Although it was not intended as such, that picture provides a beautiful illustration of God's heart for his people. So often we come to him in the hope that he will simply give us back what we have lost. The reality is so much more. Isaiah 40:31 says, 'Those who wait upon God get fresh strength. They spread their wings and soar like eagles' (MSG).

Did you know that you were born to fly?

As Jesus and his disciples left Jericho one day a commotion began. For years a blind beggar named Bartimaeus had sat in the same place at the side of the road. Watching without seeing he listened in darkness as the world went by. For so long he had been dependent on the scraps people had thrown him, defined by his blindness and powerless to change his life. Perhaps one day he began to pick out pieces of conversation: 'Jesus is coming to Jericho,' 'The teacher who heals people is travelling through here.' As he listened, hope began to grow. When he heard the large crowd that jostled past him and realized Jesus was there he began to shout. Immediately they told him to be quiet. Surely Jesus would not welcome an inter-ruption by someone like him. Ignoring the crowd he began to shout louder until the voice that others tried to silence reached the heart of God. Stopping, Jesus told the crowd to call the blind man over.

I love Bartimaeus' reaction. As a beggar with no earthly possessions, the cloak on his back would have been the only thing he had. Jumping up he threw it aside and came to Jesus. What if Jesus did not heal him? How would a blind man ever find his cloak again in that crowd? Bartimaeus was so convinced by who Jesus was that nothing was going to hold him back. He was not disappointed. Jesus not only gave Bartimaeus back his sight, he did infinitely more.

When we first met him, Bartimaeus was sitting at the side of the road, an unseeing spectator in his own world. Mark 10:52 tells us that, after Bartimaeus met Jesus, he began to follow him on the road. The fact is Bartimaeus was meant for so much more than life on the sidelines. Jesus not only gave him sight, he gave him the direction, purpose and life that enabled him to enjoy his sight to the full.

So many of us come to Jesus asking him to give us life and then go back to sit on the sidelines. Maybe we are watching with new eyes, but we are still not living the life we have been called to. If the cry of your heart is 'I was meant for more than this', it is because you were.

When the prodigal son was sitting in the pigpen, hungry and alone, was he still his father's son? Of course! Was he living in the fullness of that relationship? Far from it!

Maybe you are beginning to realize that you have never come to Jesus at all. You have never experienced his touch or asked him to give you the life you were created for, but you really want to. If that is the case, do not let the crowd stop you. You are not defined by what others see and you do not need to be held back by the things you are scared of losing. What is an old cloak compared to life as God intended? Even if everyone else is telling you to be quiet, Jesus is waiting to hear your voice.

Maybe you have encountered Jesus before. You once stood in his presence and felt the touch of his hand. Somehow, perhaps through a combination of seemingly unimportant choices, you have found yourself back on the side of the road. You can see the life you want to live but it is passing you by. Maybe, like the prodigal son, you find yourself lost in a mess of your own making and you are longing for the relationship with your father that you once enjoyed.

Wherever you find yourself, it's time to get up and get back on the road. God is not waiting to condemn you or drag you over the coals, but to remind you that you were meant for so much more. He wants to give you the family robe and show you how to wear it. He wants to put you back on your feet and teach you how to walk.

The God of heaven wants to teach you to fly.

As the people of God we have such a rich spiritual history. Through Moses, God taught the Israelites to declare his name and live his heart. As Jesus, he came and showed the world what he had always been like. In his life, he lived his word with the love that had always been behind it. In his death and resurrection, he made it possible for us to do the same. Now it is our turn.

It is our turn to take our place as people of the kingdom who accept him as their king. It is our turn to know our awesome God and follow him in obedience. It is our turn to walk with him in holiness and cultivate his heart.

What if it is true that God has placed you here at this moment, at this point in the story, for a reason? Have you ever considered that you, like Esther, were born for such a time as this? Is it possible that God placed you in your part of this broken world, with your family and friends and neighbours, with your unique personality, abilities and even weaknesses, so that you might know him and reflect his heart in the way he designed you to do? As Eugene Petersen writes, 'When we submit our lives to what we read in Scripture we find that we are not being led to see God in our stories – but our stories in God's.'[2]

What will it take for you to play your part in God's story?

- Do you need to learn obedience?
- Do you need to know what it means to fear God?
- Do you need to understand his holiness and begin to live a life that is worthy of your calling?
- Do you need to rethink the things that influence your life?
- Do you need to change the way you treat the people you love? Or the people you do not?
- Do you need to study God's word and cultivate his heart?
- Do you need to get up and get back on the road?

If you are anything like me, you will need to do all that and more. The bad news is that it will take effort. The good news is that most of the effort is not ours. God is ready to transform you into the person you were always meant to be, to recreate you as the very best version of yourself.

There will come a time when the battle for holiness will be over. The rebellion that creeps up when we least expect it will be gone. We will be like him in a way we cannot imagine. When that time comes the things we cling to now will seem trivial. When we finally see him in all his beauty, what will matter more, the things that we gave up, or the people who did not see his heart – because we did not show it to them?

Life as we know it now will not go on forever. The life that God gives will. The God who always keeps his promises has told us that he is coming back to make all things new. How will you feel when that day comes? Will you hang your head and wish you had taken the time to know him more? Or will you throw yourself at his feet, overwhelmed in the presence of the one who has been the joy of your heart?

The story we are part of is so much bigger than the lives we live from day to day and yet the role each of us has been given is vitally important. What you do and who you are really does matter on a scale you cannot imagine. It is time for us as a people with a big calling and an even bigger God to rediscover our sense of awe in his presence. It is time to know him and show the world what he is like.

It is time to live like we are part of the big story.

Discussion questions

1. Read Deuteronomy 10:12–13. What did God require of his people as they prepared to enter the land of their inheritance? To what extent does this apply to us today?

2. How would you describe your relationship with God? Have you ever intentionally placed your life in his hands, accepting what he accomplished on the cross and committing to take your place within his kingdom? If you have, are you following him on the road or watching from the sidelines?

3. What will it take for you to play your part in God's story? Who are the people he has placed you among? Do you need to make any practical changes in order to know God and live as he intended? If so, what?

4. As the people of God, what part are we called to play within his story (a) individually and (b) collectively?

I pray that out of his glorious riches he may strengthen you with power through his Spirit in your inner being, so that Christ may dwell in your hearts through faith. And I pray that you, being rooted and established in love, may have power, together with all the saints, to grasp how wide and long and high and deep is the love of Christ, and to know this love that surpasses knowledge – that you may be filled to the measure of all the fullness of God. Now to him who is able to do immeasurably more than all we ask or imagine, according to his power that is at work within us, to him be glory in the church and in Christ Jesus throughout all generations, forever and ever! Amen.

(Ephesians 3:16–21)

Notes

Introduction

1. G. K. Chesterton, *Orthodoxy* (Hodder & Stoughton 1996), p. 83.
2. I am referring here to Biblical Hebrew, rather than to modern Hebrew.
3. Chief Rabbi Jonathan Sacks refers often to this aspect of the Hebrew view of history. In *Radical Then, Radical Now*, he refers to the celebration of the feasts in particular as the supreme transformation of history into memory. Jonathan Sacks, *Radical Then, Radical Now* (London, Continuum, 2003), p. 164.

Chapter 1 – The back story

1. Craig Bartholomew and Michael Goheen, *The Drama of Scripture* (London, SPCK 2006), p. 15.
2. C. S. Lewis, *Mere Christianity* (London, HarperCollins 2002), p. 50.
3. Jonathan Sacks, *To Heal a Fractured World* (London, Continuum, 2005), p. 65.

Chapter 2 – Why bother with obedience?

1. Torah (Strongs reference 8451): Warren Baker and Eugene Carpenter, *The Complete Word Study Dictionary Old Testament* (Chattanooga, Tennessee, AMG Publishers, 2003), p. 1220.
2. Yarah (Strongs reference 3384): Warren Baker and Eugene Carpenter, *The Complete Word Study Dictionary Old Testament* (Chattanooga, Tennessee, AMG Publishers, 2003), p. 473.

3. Marvin Wilson, *Our Father Abraham* (Grand Rapids, Eerdmans), p. 136.

Chapter 4 – Fear and freedom
1. C. S. Lewis, *The Lion, the Witch and the Wardrobe* (London, Collins, 1980), p. 75.

Chapter 5 – As for me and my house
1. Despite attempts to find out more about Ruth Renkel I have been able to establish very little about her identity other than being the author of several well-known quotes.

Chapter 6 – The danger from outside
1. Matthew Henry, Matthew Henry's Complete Unabridged Commentary (www.blueletterbible.com), commentary on Matthew 24:4–31.

Chapter 7 – Living with blessing
1. Elisabeth Elliot, *Through Gates of Splendour* (London, Hodder & Stoughton, 1962), p. 23.
2. Ann Spangler and Lois Tverberg, *Sitting at the Feet of Rabbi Jesus* (Grand Rapids, Zondervan, 2009), p. 93.

Chapter 8 – The call to holiness
1. Andrew Peterson, 'Fool with a fancy guitar', from the album *Counting Stars*, © Jakedog Music 2010, quoted with permission.
2. Oswald Chambers, *My Utmost for His Highest* (Uhrichsville, OH, Barbour & Co. Inc., 1963), p. 25.

Chapter 9 – Living like you belong to God
1. Oswald Chambers, *My Utmost for His Highest* (Uhrichsville, OH, Barbour & Co. Inc., 1963), p. 51.

2. Matthew Henry, Matthew Henry's Complete Unabridged Commentary (www.blueletterbible.com), commentary on Genesis 2:23. This is a modernized version of the original text.

Chapter 10 – Choosing life

1. Oxford Dictionaries (www. oxforddictionaries.com).

Chapter 12 – The Word became flesh

1. Bruce Milne, *The Message of John* (Nottingham, IVP, 1993), p. 33.

Chapter 13 – Jesus and the law

1. Dwight A. Pryor, *Jesus, Christians and the Law* (MP3) (Centre for Judaic-Christian Studies), www.jcstudies.com
2. Dwight A. Pryor, *Jesus, Christians and the Law* (MP3) (Centre for Judaic-Christian Studies), www.jcstudies.com

Chapter 16 – Joining the Haverim

1. Ann Spangler and Lois Tverberg, *Sitting at the Feet of Rabbi Jesus* (Grand Rapids, Zondervan, 2009), Chapter 5.
2. I have found the material produced by Precept Upon Precept extremely helpful. The original idea for this book was born out of the Precept Upon Precept study on Deuteronomy.

Chapter 17 – For such a time as this

1. Andrew Peterson, 'Little boy heart alive', from the album *The Far Country*, © Jakedog Music 2005, quoted with permission.
2. Eugene Petersen, *The Invitation* (NavPress, 2008), p. 11.